BIOLOGICAL REPORT 85(1.14)
APRIL 1988

Contaminant Hazard Reviews
REPORT NO. 14

LEAD HAZARDS TO FISH, WILDLIFE, AND INVERTEBRATES:
A SYNOPTIC REVIEW

by

Ronald Eisler

U.S. Fish and Wildlife Service
Patuxent Wildlife Research Center
Laurel, MD 20708

SUMMARY

Lead (Pb) and its compounds have been known to man for about 7,000 years, and Pb poisoning has been recognized for at least 2,500 years. All credible evidence indicates that Pb is neither essential nor beneficial to living organisms, and that all measured effects are adverse--including those on survival, growth, reproduction, development, behavior, learning, and metabolism.

Various living resources are at increased risk from Pb: migratory waterfowl that frequent hunted areas and ingest shot; avian predators that eat game wounded by hunters; domestic livestock near smelters, refineries, and Pb battery recycling plants; captive zoo animals and domestic livestock held in enclosures coated with Pb-based paints; wildlife that forage extensively near heavily traveled roads; aquatic life in proximity to mining activities, areas where Pb arsenate pesticides are used, metal finishing industries, organolead industries, and areas of Pb aerosol fallout; and crops and invertebrates growing or living in Pb-contaminated soils.

Adverse effects on aquatic biota reported at waterborne Pb concentrations of 1.0 to 5.1 ug/l included reduced survival, impaired reproduction, reduced growth, and high bioconcentration from the medium. Among sensitive species of birds, survival was reduced at doses of 50 to 75 mg Pb^{2+}/kg body weight (BW) or 28 mg organolead/kg BW, reproduction was impaired at dietary levels of 50 mg Pb /kg, and signs of poisoning were evident at doses as low as 2.8 mg organolead/kg BW. In general, forms of Pb other than shot (or ingestible Pb objects), or routes of administration other than ingestion, are unlikely to cause clinical signs of Pb poisoning in birds. Data for toxic and sublethal effects of Pb on mammalian wildlife are missing. For sensitive species of domestic and laboratory animals, survival was reduced at acute oral Pb doses of 5 mg/kg BW (rat), at chronic oral doses of 5 mg/kg BW (dog), and at dietary levels of 1.7 mg/kg BW (horse). Sublethal effects were documented in monkeys exposed to doses as low as 0.1 mg Pb/kg BW daily (impaired learning at 2 years postadministration) or fed diets containing 0.5 mg Pb/kg (abnormal social behavior). Signs of Pb exposure were recorded in rabbits given 0.005 mg Pb/kg BW and in mice given 0.05 mg Pb/kg BW. Tissue Pb levels were elevated in mice given doses of 0.03 mg Pb/kg BW, and in sheep given 0.05 mg Pb/kg BW. In general, organolead compounds were more toxic than inorganic Pb compounds, food chain biomagnification of Pb vas negligible, and younger organisms were most susceptible. More research seems merited on organolead toxicokinetics (including effects on behavior and learning), and on mammalian wildlife sensitivity to Pb and its compounds.

Recent legislation limiting the content of Pb in paints, reducing the Pb content in gasoline, and eliminating the use of Pb shot nationwide (Pb shot phaseout program/schedule starting in 1986, and fully implemented by 1991) in waterfowl hunting areas will substantially reduce environmental burdens of Pb and may directly benefit sensitive fishery and wildlife resources. Continued nationwide monitoring of Pb in living resources is necessary in order to correlate reduced emission sources with reduced tissue Pb concentrations.

Suggested citation for this report:

Eisler, R. 1988. Lead hazards to fish, wildlife, and invertebrates: a synoptic review. U.S. Fish Wildl. Serv. Biol. Rep. 85(1.14).

TABLES

ACKNOWLEDGMENTS

I thank Nancy A. Bushby, Lynda J. Garrett, and Joyce E. Haber for technical services; Julia Armstrong and Jean Higgis for secretarial help; Louis N. Locke, Jerry R. Longcore, Keith A. Morehouse, Oliver H. Pattee, Matthew C. Perry, and Christopher J, Schmitt for reviewing the manuscript; and Paul H. Eschmeyer and James R. Zuboy for editorial services.

INTRODUCTION

Lead (Pb) has been known for centuries to be a cumulative metabolic poison; however, acute exposure is lessening. Of greater concern is the possibility that continuous exposure to low concentrations of the metal as a result of widespread environmental contamination may result in adverse health effects (Nriagu 1978b). Environmental pollution from Pb is now so high that body burdens in the general human population are closer than the burdens of any other toxic chemical to those that produce clinical poisoning (Hejtmancik et al. 1982). Further, Pb is a mutagen and teratogen when absorbed in excessive amounts, has carcinogenic or cocarcinogenic properties, impairs reproduction and liver and thyroid functions, and interferes with resistance to infectious diseases (EPA 1979).

Ecological and toxicological aspects of lead and its compounds in the environment have been extensively reviewed. (Wetmore (1919); Bellrose (1959), Aronson (1971), Barth et al. (1973), NRCC (1973), Holl and Hampp (1975), Boggess (1977), Rolfe and Reinbold (1977), Forbes and Sanderson (1978), Nriagu (1978a, 1978b), Wong et al. (1978), CEP (1979), EPA. (1979, 1980, 1985), Levander (1979), Tsuchiya (1979), Branica and Konrad (1980), Jenkins (1980) NAS (1980), Eisler (1981), Harrison and Laxen (1981), Demayo et al. (1982), Mudge (1983), De Michele (1984), Feierabend and Myers (1984), Walsh and Tilson (1984), Lumeij (1985), Feierabend and Russell (1986), FWS (1986a), Kania and Nash (1986), Lansdown and Yule (1986), McDonald (1986), Sanderson and Bellrose (1986), Pain (1987). There is agreement by all authorities on five points. First, Pb is ubiquitous and is a characteristic trace constituent in rocks, soils, water, plants, animals, and air. Second, more than 4 million metric tons of Pb are produced worldwide each year, mostly for the manufacture of storage batteries, gasoline additives, pigments, alloys, and ammunition. The widespread broadcasting of Pb through anthropogenic activities, especially during the past 40 years, has resulted in an increase in Pb residues throughout the environment--an increase that has dislocated the equilibrium of the biogeochemical cycle of Pb. Third, Pb is neither essential nor beneficial to living organisms; all existing data show that its metabolic effects are adverse. Fourth, Pb is toxic in most of its chemical forms and can be incorporated into the body by inhalation, ingestion, dermal absorption, and placental transfer to the fetus. Fifth, Pb is an accumulative metabolic poison that affects behavior, as well as the hematopoietic, vascular, nervous, renal, and reproductive systems. In humans, Pb causes stillbirths, miscarriages, inhibited development of fetuses, decreased male fertility, and abnormal sperm. Severe damage to the central nervous system from exposure to large amounts of Pb may result in stupor, convulsions, coma, and death. Children that survive Pb poisoning are often permanently retarded or have permanent neurological handicaps. At subclinical injury levels, Pb causes slight, but irreversible, damage to the brain development of growing children.

Natural resources are also affected by environmental Pb contamination, and some wildlife species numbers may be reduced as a result. For example, waterfowl deaths resulting from the ingestion of spent Pb shot pellets from shotgun shells were discovered more than 100 years ago in Italy and in the United States; since then Pb poisoning of waterfowl has occurred in 15 countries (Street 1983). In North America alone, approximately 3,000 tons of Pb shot are expended annually into lakes, marshes, and estuaries by several million waterfowl hunters (FWS 1986, 1987). Spent pellets are eaten by waterfowl and other birds, either in mistake for seeds or as pieces of grit. These pellets may be retained in the gizzard for weeks, where they are reduced chemically and mechanically, form soluble toxic salts, and cause characteristic signs of Pb intoxication--especially lethargy and emaciation (Street 1983). At least 2% of all North American waterfowl--or about 2 million ducks and geese (Lumeij 1985)--die each year as a direct result of ingestion of Pb shot (Bellrose 195!). These deaths contribute to the decline of some species, such as the canvasback, *Aythya valisineria* (Dieter 1979), pintail, *Anas acuta* (White and Stendell 1977), and black duck, *Anas rubripes* (Pain and Rattner 1988). Up to 7X more waterfowl died from Pb toxicosis as a result of ingesting spent pellets than from wounding by hunters (Zwank et al. 1985). In addition, Pb-poisoned waterfowl show delayed mortality from Pb-induced starvation, are readily captured by predators, are susceptible to disease, and reproduce poorly (Dieter 1979). Susceptibility is markedly influenced by species, by the number and size of shot ingested, and by the types of foods eaten (White and Stendell 1977). Swans are among the more vulnerable waterfowl. In England, Pb poisoning through the ingestion of discarded Pb fishing sinkers is the major cause of death in the mute swan, *Cygnus olor* (Birkhead 1983); for all species of swans in England, about half died as a direct result of Pb poisoning (Demayo et al. 1982). In Washington State, 30% of the endangered trumpeter swans (*Cygnus buccinator*) found dead had died of Pb poisoning from ingestion of Pb shot (Kendall and Driver 1982). Lead toxicosis caused by ingestion of spent shot and other Pb objects has also been reported for sandhill crane, *Grus canadensis* (Windingstad et al. 1984); Canada goose, *Branta canadensis* (Szymczak and Adrian 1978); mourning dove, *Zenaidura macroura* (Locke and Bagley

1967); and wild turkey, *Meleagris gallopavo* (Stone and Butkas 1978). Secondary poisoning has been documented in at least five species of raptors that ate food containing Pb shot (especially hunter-wounded animals): Andean condor, *Vultur gryphus* (Locke et al. 1969); bald eagle, *Haliaeetus leucocephalus* (Pattee and Hennes 1983); honey buzzard, *Pernis apivorus* (Lumeij et al. 1985); king vulture, *Sarcorhampus papa* (Decker et al 1979); and California condor *Gymnogyps californianus* (Janssen et al. 1986).

The availability of Pb-based paints, discarded oil filters, used crankcase oil, Pb storage batteries, or pastures contaminated by industrial lead operations make Pb one of the most common causes of accidental poisoning in domestic animals (Demayo et al. 1982). Cattle and horses in the vicinity of a Pb smelter in California developed signs of Pb poisoning, and many died between 1880, when the smelter opened, and 1971, when the smelter closed (Burrows 1981). Of the mules used in the early mining of Pb, all died during their first year of service (Burrows 1981). Lead toxicosis has been reported in buffalos and cattle in India after they ate green fodder near a factory that recycled Pb from old batteries (Kwatra et al. 1986). Total milk yield declined sharply, and stillbirths and abortions increased significantly in cattle that ingested Pb-contaminated hay; the field from which the hay had been cut had a history of use for clay pigeon shoots and contained an estimated 3.6 tons of Pb shot pellets (Frape and Pringle 1984). In sheep grazing in areas near Pb mines, the frequency of abortions was high, and the learning behavior of the lambs was impaired (Demayo et al. 1982). Many species of zoo animals, including monkeys, fruit-eating bats, and parrots, have been fatally poisoned from ingestion of flaking Pb-based paint on the walls and bars of their cages (NRC 1973). Ingestion of Pb-based paint chips was one cause of epizootic mortality of fledgling Laysan albatross, *Diomedea immutabilis*, at Midway Atoll in 1983 (Sileo and Fefer 1987). At present, there is no known dietary requirement for Pb in domestic animals, nor has it been shown unequivocally that Pb plays any beneficial role (NRCC 1973). On the contrary, Pb demonstrably and adversely affects weight, survival, behavior, litter size, and skeletal development (Tsuchiya 1979), and induces teratogenic and carcinogenic responses in some species of experimental animals (NRCC 1973; EPA 1980).

Lead is not essential for plants, and excessive amounts can cause growth inhibition, as well as reduced photosynthesis, mitosis, and water absorption (Demayo et al. 1982). The decline of some European spruce forests has been attributed to excessive concentrations of atmospheric Pb (Backhaus and Backhaus 1986).

Lead is toxic to all phyla of aquatic biota, though effects are modified significantly by various biological and abiotic variables (Wong et al. 1978). Wastes from Pb mining activities have severely reduced or eliminated populations of fish and aquatic invertebrates, either directly through lethal toxicity or indirectly through toxicity to prey species (Demayo et al. 1982). Health advisories warning anglers against eating Pb-contaminated fish have been posted in Missouri (Schmitt and Finger 1987). The significant increases in Pb concentration shown by marine corals between 1954 and 1980 were representative of the increases noted in other biota as a direct result of increased global Pb availability during that period (Dodge and Gilbert 1984).

In this report, I summarize available data on lead in the environment, with emphasis on fishery and wildlife resources, and review current recommendations for the protection of sensitive species. This account is part of a continuing series of brief, reviews prepared in response to requests for information from environmental specialists of the U.S. Fish and Wildlife Service.

SOURCES AND USES

Lead is a comparatively rare metal, with an average abundance in the earth's crust of 16 mg/kg (EPA 1980); it is also a major constituent of more than 200 identified minerals, of which only 3 are sufficiently abundant to form mineral deposits (EPA 1980): galena (PbS), angelesite ($PbSO_4$), and cerusite ($PbCO_3$). Galena, the primary form of Pb in the natural state, is often associated with sphalerite (ZnS), pyrite (FeS_2), chalcopyrite ($CuFeS_2$), and other sulfur salts (May and McKinney 1981). Most (88 %) of the domestic primary Pb production originates from stratabound deposits in southeastern Missouri, another 8% from Idaho's Couer D'Alene district, and the rest from deposits in Colorado and Utah. Primary Pb is smelted and refined at plants in Texas, Montana, Nebraska, Missouri, and Idaho. Scrap Pb, or secondary Pb, accounted for about half the domestic consumption in 1978; by 1980, more Pb was produced from secondary sources than from domestic ores (May and McKinney 1981).

About 4 million tons of Pb are refined annually worldwide (Table 1) Domestic Pb consumption is 1.3 million tons annually, of which about half is used in storage battery manufacture and, until recently, about 20% in the manufacture of gasoline antiknock additives such as tetramethyllead (TML) and tetraethyllead (TEL) (Table 2). Pigments and ceramics account for about 6% of consumption, and metallic Pb products, Pb-containing alloys, paint, solder, and ammunition constitute other minor use categories (EPA 1980). Lead enters the atmosphere mainly through smelter emissions, primarily as $PbSO_4$ and $PbO- PbSO_4$, and through vehicle emissions, which include unburned Pb, TEL, TML, and various Pb halides, sulfates, phosphates, and oxides (Harrison and Laxen 1981).

Lead and its compounds have been known to man for about 7,000 years, and Pb poisoning has occurred for at least 2,500 years (Barth et al. 1973). In Egypt, between 5,000 and 7,000 BC, Pb was used for glazing pottery, solder, ornaments, net sinker, anchors, caulking, coins, weights, aqueducts, piping, and cooking utensils (Nriagu 1978a). The biocidal properties of Pb were familiar to the ancient Egyptians, and Pb salts were sometimes used by them for homicidal purposes (De Michele 1984). Lead encephalopathy (inflammation of the brain) has been recognized since 400 BC among workers in the Pb trades; initial symptoms are dullness, irritability, ataxia, headaches, memory loss, and restlessness. These symptoms often progressed to delirium, mania, coma, convulsions, and sometimes death. The same general effects were described in young children and infants, among which mortality was sometimes 40% (EPA 1980). Extensive use of Pb by the Romans, circa 500, in pipes for water transport, in cosmetics, and as a wine sweetener (Harrison and Laxen 1981), is estimated to have increased environmental Pb levels to about 5X the existing background levels (Eisenreich et al. 1986). The decline of the Roman Empire may have been hastened by endemic lead poisoning--a theory supported by residue data showing high Pb concentrations in bones and remains of Roman aristocrats (Nriagu 1978a)--perhaps through ingestion of excessive amounts of wine laced with Pb (De Michele 1984). After the fall of the Romans, the use of Pb declined sharply. In the 14th century, gunpowder was introduced into Europe and was the impetus for the development of a weapon that fired a malleable metal pellet: a lead shot (EPA 1979). Otherwise, the metal's resistance to corrosion led to its use as lead sheets applied as roofing for cathedrals and as protective encasement of underground pillars. In 1721, the first Pb mine was established in the New World by English settlers at Falling Creek, Virginia, primarily to supply bullets and shot (EPA 1979). By 1750, European and British Pb smelting operations were flourishing (Nriagu 1978a). In 1763, Pb deposits in southeastern Missouri were permanently opened (EPA 1979). The 18th century's Industrial Revolution produced an estimated 10-fold increase in existing Pb background levels (Eisenreich et al. 1986). In the late 1700's, symptoms of acute Pb poisoning recorded among industrial workers were called "Mill Reek" or "Devonshire Colic" (NRCC 1973). Lead poisoning was frequently recorded among U.S. lead miners in 1870-1900, especially in Utah, Colorado, and New Mexico. By 1880, the United States had surpassed Germany and Spain in the mining and refining of Pb, and has continued as the leader in the output of refined Pb (EPA 1979). Air pollution from combustion of leaded gasoline containing TEL rose in the 1920's (NRCC 1973). In the mid-1940's, atmospheric Pb concentrations increased sharply due to massive increases in Pb emissions from automobiles; since then, increased Pb emissions to the atmosphere have matched trends in gasoline Pb content and consumption (Eisenreich et al. 1986; Smith et al. 1987). In 1957, the United States was overtaken by Australia and the USSR in domestic mine production of Pb; however, in 1967, the opening of the "New Lead Belt" in Missouri revived mining in the United States, and subsequently Pb was produced at the annual rate of 450,000 to 550,000 metric tons (EPA 1979). In 1975, the United States was again the leading Pb producer from mine sources, accounting for 16% of the world total; at that time, about 70% of the world Pb production came from the USA, the USSR, Australia, Canada, Peru, Mexico, China, Yugoslavia, and Bulgaria (Tsuchiya 1979,). In 1986, world mine production of lead was 2,352,000 tons of which USA mine production was 353,000 tons, or 15% of the world total, and production in Missouri was 308,000 tons, or 87% of the USA total (personal communication, R. L. Amistadi, Doe Run Company, St. Louis, Missouri).

Table 1. World Pb production, consumption, and principal end uses (modified from Harrison and Laxen 1981; Demayo et al. 1982).

Production consumption, and use	Metric tons, in thousands
Production, 1978	
Mined Pb	3,625
Refined Pb	4,202
Consumption	
1977	2,995
1980	3,801
Principal end uses of refined Pb	
1977	
Storage batteries	1,478
Pigments and chemicals	369
Tetraalkyllead	292
Cable covering	216
Pipe and sheeting	160
Other	480
1980	
Storage batteries	1,330
Tetraethyllead	380
Cable covering	380
Solder	380
Litharge	190
Building construction	190
Caulking	190
Other	760

Table 2. Use patterns for Pb in selected countries (from EPA 1979).

Use	USA		Europe[a]		Japan	
Storage batteries	613	(47)	392	(34)	93	(40)
Cable sheathing	14	(1)	145	(13)	16	(7)
Pigments and chemicals	303	(23)	294	(26)	62	(27)
Alloys	75	(6)	50	(4)	15	(7)
Ammunition	66	(5)	b	(-)	b	(-)
Other	226	(18)	267	(23)	44	(19)
Total	1,297		1,148		230	

Thousands of metric tons (percent)

[a] France, West Germany, Italy, UK

[b] Not reported.

CHEMICAL PROPERTIES

Elemental Pb is a bluish-gray, soft metal of atomic weight 207.19 and atomic number 82; it melts at 327.5 C, boils at 1,749 C, and has a density of 11.34 g/cm^3 at 25°C. Metallic Pb is sparingly soluble in hard, basic waters to 30 ug/l, and up to 500 ug/l in soft, acidic waters. Lead has four stable isotopes: Pb-204 (1.5%), Pb-206 (23.6%), Pb-207 (22.6%), and Pb-208 (52.3%). Of its 24 radioactive isotopes, two (Pb-210, Tb 1/2 of 22 years; Pb-212, Tb ½ of 10 hours) have been used in tracer experiments. Lead occurs in four valence states: elemental (Pb^0), monovalent (Pb^+), divalent (Pb^{2+}), and tetravalent (Pb^{4+}); all forms are environmentally important, except possibly Pb^+. In nature, lead occurs mainly as Pb^{2+}; it is oxidized to Pb^{4+} only under strong oxidizing conditions, and few simple compounds of Pb^{4+} other than PbO_2 are stable. Some Pb salts are comparatively soluble in water (lead acetate, 443 g/l; lead nitrate, 565 g/l; lead chloride, 9.9 g/1), whereas others are only sparingly soluble (lead sulfate, 42.5 mg/l; lead oxide, 17 mg/l; lead sulfide, 0.86 mg/1); solubility is greatest at elevated temperatures in the range 0 to 40° C. Of the organoleads, tetraethyllead (TEL) and tetramethyllead (TML) are the most stable and the most important because of their widespread use as antiknock fuel additives. Both are clear, colorless, volatile liquids, highly soluble in many organic solvents; however, solubility in water is only 0.18 mg/l for TEL, and 18.0 mg/l for TML. Boiling points are 199° C for TEL and 110 C for TML; both undergo photochemical degradation in the atmosphere to elemental Pb and free organic radicals, although the fate of automotive organoleads has yet to be fully evaluated. Additional information on the general chemistry of lead and its compounds was reviewed by NRCC (1973), Boggess (1977), Nriagu (1978a), EPA (1979, 1980), Tsuchiya (1979), Harrison and Laxen (1981), and Demayo et al. (1982).

Lead chemistry is complex. In water, for example, Pb is most soluble and bioavailable under conditions of low pH, low organic content, low concentrations of suspended sediments, and low concentrations of the salts of calcium, iron, manganese, zinc, and cadmium. Accordingly, solubility of lead is low in water, except in areas of local point source discharges (Harrison and Laxen 1981; Scoullos 1986). Lead and its compounds tend to concentrate in the water surface microlayer (i.e., the upper 0.3 mm), especially when surface organic materials are present in thin films (Demayo et al. 1982). Organolead compounds are generally of anthropogenic origin and are found mostly in the aquatic environment as contaminants; however, some organolead complexes form naturally, and their rate of formation may be affected by man-made organoleads (Nriagu 1978a). In surface waters, Pb exists in three forms: dissolved labile (e.g., Pb^{2+}, $PbOH^+$, $PBCO_3$), dissolved bound (e.g., colloids or strong complexes), or as a particulate (Benes et al. 1985). The labile forms represent a significant part of the Pb input from washout of atmospheric deposits, whereas particulate and bound forms were common in urban runoff and ore-mining effluents (Benes et al. 1985). The solubility of Pb compounds in water is pH dependent, and ranges from about 10 g Pb/1 at pH 5.5, to less than 1 ug Pb/1 at pH 9.0 (EPA 1980); little detectable Pb remains in solution at pH >8.0 (Prause et al. 1985). At pH 6.5 and water alkalinity of 25 mg $CaCO_3/1$, elemental Pb is soluble to 330 ug/l; however, Pb under the same conditions is soluble to 1,000 ug/l (Demayo et al. 1982). In acidic waters, the common forms of dissolved Pb are salts of $PbSO_4$ and $PbCl_4$, ionic Pb, cationic forms of lead hydroxide, and (to a lesser extent) the ordinary hydroxide $Pb(OH)_2$. In alkaline waters, common species include the anionic forms of Pb carbonate and hydroxide, and the hydroxide species present in acidic waters (NRCC 1973). Unfortunately, the little direct information available about the speciation of Pb in natural aqueous solutions has seriously limited our understanding of Pb transport and removal mechanisms (Nriagu 1978a).

Most Pb entering natural waters is precipitated to the sediment bed as carbonates or hydroxides (May and McKinney 1981). Lead is readily precipitated by many common anions; desorption and replacement by other cations is extremely slow (Boggess 1977). In some acidic lakes, the deposition of particulate Pb was strongly correlated with the deposition of aluminum and carbon, especially during periods of increasing pH (White and Driscoll 1985). Precipitation of sparingly soluble Pb compounds is not a primary factor controlling the concentration of dissolved Pb in stream waters. Migration and speciation of Pb was strongly affected by water flow rate, increasing flow rate resulting in increased concentrations of particulate and labile Pb and a decrease in bound forms. At low stream flow, Pb was rapidly removed from the water column by sedimentation (Benes et al. 1985).

In the sediments, Pb is mobilized and released when the pH decreases suddenly or ionic composition changes (Demayo et al. 1982). However, there was no significant release of Pb from dredge spoils suspended in estuarine waters of different salinities for 4 weeks (Prause et al. 1985). Some Pb^{2+} in sediments may be transformed to tetraalkyllead compounds, including TML, through chemical and microbial processes. There is also the possibility of methylation of ionic Pb in vivo by fish and other aquatic biota, but the mechanisms are unclear (May and McKinney 1981). Methylation of Pb in sediments was positively related to increasing temperatures, reduced pH, and microbial activity, but seemed to be independent of Pb concentration (Demayo et al. 1982). In general, the concentration of tetraalkylleads in sediments is low, representing less than 10% of total Pb (Chau et al. 1980).

MODE OF ACTION

Lead modifies the function and structure of kidney, bone, the central nervous system, and the hematopoietic system and produces adverse biochemical, histopathological, neuropsychological, fetotoxic, teratogenic, and reproductive effects (Boggess 1977; Nriagu 1978b; De Michele 1984). Inorganic Pb absorbed into the mammalian body enters the bloodstream initially and attaches to the red blood cell. There is a further rapid distribution of the Pb between blood extracellular fluid and other storage sites that is so rapid that only about half the freshly absorbed Pb remains in the blood after a few minutes. The storage sites for Pb are uncertain, although they are probably in soft tissues as well as bone; the half-time residence life (Tb 1/2) of inorganic Pb is estimated to be 20 days in blood, 28 days in whole body, and 600 to 3,000 days in bone (Harrison and Laxen 1981). Inorganic Pb in the environment can be biologically methylated to produce alkyllead compounds (Walsh and Tilson 1984). Bile is an important route of excretion; ingested Pb probably proceeds sequentially from gut, to blood, to bone and soft tissue, and by way of the bile to small intestine and fecal excretion (De Michele 1984).

Tetraalkyllead mode of action differs from that of inorganic Pb. Although initial entry is still into the bloodstream, the Pb is evenly distributed between blood plasma and the red blood cells. Tetraalkylleads are lost rapidly from the bloodstream, although some reappear in 5 to 10 hours associated exclusively with the red blood cells, probably as trialkyllead, though a fraction may be converted to inorganic Pb. The organoleads concentrate in liver, and it is there that tetraalkyllead is probably converted to trialkyllead. Otherwise, the Pb is widely dispersed throughout the body with Tb 1/2 values of 200 to 350 days (Harrison and Laxen 1981). Tetraethyllead, by virtue of its liposolubility, is rapidly accumulated in nonbony tissues, particularly the brain, where the onset of signs of poisoning is rapid (Nriagu 1978b). Short-term repeated exposures of rats (*Rattus* spp.) to TEL results in a neurotoxic syndrome consisting of altered reactivity to noxious stimulation through disruption of forebrain-area function (Hong et al 1983). Several fish species metabolize tetraalkylleads to trialkyllead compounds by way of their mixed function oxidase system (Wong et al. 1981). The trialkyllead derivatives are considered responsible for the toxicity of the parent compound (Walsh and Tilson 1984). Trialkylleads and dialkylleads rapidly traverse biological membranes in bird eggs and accumulate in the yolk and developing embryo (Forsyth et al. 1985). At present, the organolead mode of action is poorly understood, but organolead compounds are known to inhibit amino acid transport, uncouple oxidative phosphorylation, and inhibit cerebral glucose metabolism (Hong et al. 1983).

Biochemically, Pb exerts deleterious effects on hematopoiesis through derangement of hemoglobin synthesis, resulting in a shortened life span of circulating erythrocytes, often resulting in anemia. Two essential enzymes in heme formation that are extremely sensitive to Pb are delta aminolevulinic acid dehydratase (ALAD), which catalyzes the dehydration of delta amino levulinic acid (ALA) to form porphobilinogen (PBG), and ferrochelatase (= heme synthetase), which catalyzes the insertion of Fe^{2+} into protoporphyrin IX (PP). This second reaction requires the presence of glutathione and ascorbic acid. Some of the intermediates in heme follow sequentially: ALA, PBG, uroporphyrinogen III, coproporphyrinogen III, protoporphyrinogen IX, and PP. It is now well established that ALAD and ferrochelatase are the most sensitive biochemical indicators of Pb exposure, the net result being lowered ALAD activity and elevated PP activity (Barth et al. 1973; Nriagu 1978b; EPA 1979, 1980; Tsuchiya 1979; Harrison and Laxen 1981; Hoffman et al. 1981; De Michele 1984; Schmitt et al. 1984; Lumeij 1985).

Inhibition of blood ALAD activity after exposure to Pb has been documented in many species of freshwater and marine teleosts (Hodson 1976; Hodson et al. 1977, 1980; Johansson-Sjobeck and Larsson 1979; Krajnovic-Ozretic and Ozretic 1980; Demayo et al. 1982; Schmitt et al. 1984; Haux et al. 1986), in the freshwater cladoceran, *Daphnia magna* (Berglind et al. 1985), in ducks, quail, doves, swallows, raptors, and songbirds

9

(Finley et al. 1976.; Dieter and Finley 1978; Dieter 1979; Hoffman et al. 1981; Franson and Custer 1982; Kendall et al. 1982; Kendall and Scanlon 1982; Eastin et al. 1983; Franson et al. 1983; Hoffman et al. 1985a, 1985b; Beyer et al. 1988), and in humans, sheep, mice, rats, rabbits, and calves (Barth et al. 1973; Boggess 1977; Nriagu 1978b; Tsuchiya 1979; Hejtmancik et al. 1982; Hayashi 1983; Peter and Strunc 1983; Schlick et al. 1983; Gietzen and Wooley 1984; Zmudzki et al. 1984). Lead-induced ALAD inhibition has been recorded not only in blood, but also in brain, spleen, liver, kidney, and bone marrow (Johansson-Sjobeck and Larsson 1979; Hoffman et al. 1981, 1985a, 1985b; Schlick et al. 1983; Friend 1985). Time for ALAD recovery to normal levels is dose dependent, organ specific, and usually directly correlated with blood Pb concentrations (Finley et al. 1976; Hodson et al. 1977; Dieter 1979; Hayashi 1983; Friend 1985). ALAD activity levels in Pb-stressed teleosts were normal 3 to 11.7 weeks postadministration (Hodson et al. 1977; Johansson-Sjobeck and Larsson 1979; Krajnovic-Ozretic and Ozretic 1980; Demayo et al. 1982); this range was 2 to 14 weeks in birds (Dieter and Finley 1978; Kendall et al. 1982; Kendall and Scanlon 1982; Friend 1985), and 3 to 12 weeks in mammals (Barth et al. 1973; Schlick et al. 1983). The physiological significance of depressed blood ALAD activity levels, except perhaps as an early indicator of Pb exposure, is debatable. Aside from a few instances of moderate anemia in workers at lead smelters, other abnormalities noted were not regarded as serious (Barth et al. 1973 Lead-induced depression in ALAD activity in mallard (*Anas platyrhynchos* ducklings and ring-necked pheasant (*Phasianus colchicus*) chicks was not associated with signs of overt toxicity (Eastin et a . 1983); a similar case is made for Pb-stressed domestic chickens (*Gallus* sp.) showing 98% reduction in ALAD activity (Franson and Custer 1982), and for American kestrel (*Falco sparverius*) showing an 80% reduction (Franson et al. 1983). Birds may be more sensitive than mammals to Pb-induced depressions in blood ALAD activity (Dieter et al. 1976). In ducks, for example, inhibition of ALAD would be more harmful than a comparable depression in mammals, for three reasons (Dieter et al. 1976). First, metabolic activity is greater in nucleated duck erythrocytes than in human erythrocytes. Second, ducks require porphyrin synthesis not only for hemoglobin production (as in humans), but also for production of respiratory heme-containing enzymes. Finally, the half-life of erythrocytes is shorter in ducks than in humans: 40 days vs. 120 days.

Elevated blood protoporphyrin IX activity resulting from Pb-inhibition of heme synthetase has been documented for humans and small mammals (Peter and Strunc 1983) and for many species of birds (Anders et al. 1982; Carlson and Nielsen 1985; Friend 1985; Franson et al. 1986; Beyer et al. 1988); recovery to normal levels occurs in a Pb-free environment in 2 to 7 weeks. Franson et al. (1986) endorsed the blood protoporphyrin IX technique instead of ALAD as a means of measuring Pb stress because of its comparative simplicity and lower cost.

Other chemical changes that have been observed as a result of Pb exposure include increased serum creatinine and serum alanine aminotransferase in birds, suggestive of kidney and liver alterations (Hoffman et al. 1981); changes in potassium, chloride, and glucose metabolism in rainbow trout, *Salmo gairdneri* (Haux and Larsson 1982); and a decrease in brain acetylcholinesterase activity in rats (Gietzen and Wooley 1984).

In kidney, Pb tends to accumulate in the proximal convoluted tubule cells of the renal cortex, producing morphological changes such as interstitial fibrosis, edema, and acid-fast intranuclear inclusion bodies, as well as biochemical changes (Locke et al. 1966; Boggess 1977; Nriagu 1978b; EPA 1980; De Michele 1984). Renal intranuclear inclusion bodies occurred in 83% of mallards experimentally poisoned by dietary Pb acetate or Pb shot (Beyer et al. 1988); similar results have been reported in other species of birds (Clemens et al. 1975; Anders et al. 1982) and in primates, cattle, and bats (Zook et al. 1972; Osweiler and Van Gelder 1978; Colle et al. 1980; Tachon et al. 1983).

In the cladoceran *Daphnia magna,* about 90% of the total body Pb burden is adsorbed to the exoskeleton (Berglind et al. 1985). In animals with a vertebral column, total amounts of Pb tend to increase with age; by far the most Pb is bound to the skeleton, especially in areas of active bone formation (Barth et al. 1973; Tsuchiya 1979; EPA 1980; Hejtmancik et al. 1982; Mykkanen et al. 1982; Peter and Strunc 1983; De Michele 1984; Eisler 1984; Berglind et al. 1985; Marcus 1985). The retention of Pb stored in bone pools poses a number of difficulties for the usual multicompartmental loss-rate models. Some Pb in bones of high medullary content, such as the femur and sternum, have relatively long retention times--i.e., Tb 1/2 of >20 years in humans-- whereas Pb stored in bones of low medullary content have Tb 1/2 values of 20 to 200 days, similar to the values for Pb in soft tissues and blood (Tsuchiya 1979; Marcus 1985). In birds, medullary bone undergoes sequences of bone formation and destruction associated with the storage and liberation of calcium during eggshell formation, indicating that sex and physiological condition primarily influence Pb kinetics in avian bone (Finley and Dieter 1978). Marcus (1985) endorsed the use of diffusion models based on the exchange of Pb between blood in canaliculi and the crystalline bone of the osteon to account for retention and bioavailability. More research is needed on the role of bone in Pb kinetics.

Lead damages nerve cells and ganglia, and alters cell structure and enzyme function. Axonal degenerative changes, especially in neuronal cell bodies, were recorded in Pb-poisoned freshwater snails (*Viviparous ater*), leading to altered protein synthesis (Fantin et al. 1985). Mallards dosed orally with Pb shot developed demyelinating lesions in vagal, branchial, and sciatic nerves, and showed vascular damage in the cerebellum; lesions were similar to those in Pb-intoxicated guinea pigs (*Cavia* sp.), rats, and guinea hens, *Gallus* sp. (Hunter and Wobeser 1980). Crop stasis in birds, which is characterized by paralysis of the alimentary tract, impaction of food in the gizzard and proventriculus, and regurgitation of crop fluid, has been produced by Pb shot or Pb acetate solutions. Lead induces crop dysfunction by acting either directly on the smooth muscle or on associated nerve plexuses of crop tissue, depending on the route of administration (Clemens et al. 1975; Boyer et al. 1985; Boyer and Di Stefano 1985). Mammals, including humans, undergo similar alimentary distress following intakes of lead (Boyer et al. 1985).

Effects of Pb on the nervous system are both structural and functional, involving the cerebellum, spinal cord, and motor and sensory nerves; the result may be deterioration of intellectual, sensory, neuromuscular, and psychological functions (Nraigu 1978b). The pathogenesis of Pb-induced injury to the nervous system is poorly understood, but may be mediated through vascular damage, the direct action of Pb on neurons, or alterations in porphyrin metabolism (Hunter and Wobeser 1980). Retarded brain growth in prenatal guinea pigs has been recorded at subclinical levels of Pb (i.e., at concentrations producing no elevation in blood Pb and no change in body weight), and this effect is potentiated at temperatures of 42° C (Edwards and Beatson 1984). Lead may cause a transient disturbance in the blood-brain barrier during early postnatal growth of rats. This effect is associated with the presence of hemorrhagic lesions, suggesting focal damage to the vessels as an important event in the pathogenesis of Pb encephalopathy to suckling rats (Sundstrom et al. 1985). Brain histopathology has been recorded in Pb-poisoned chickens (Narbaitz et al. 1985) and cattle (Osweiler and Van Gelder 1978). Brain Pb concentrations are usually among the lowest in body organs, but the brain is one of the main sites of action. During chronic Pb poisoning, distribution of Pb in the brain is positively related to both dose and duration of exposure; preferential accumulation is in the hippocampus area of the brain. Significant amounts of Pb persisted in rat brain tissue up to 4 weeks after the withdrawal of Pb treatment (Collins et al. 1982). The role of organolead compounds in hippocampal function is largely unknown (Czech and Hoium 1984).

Absorption and retention of Pb from the gastrointestinal tract, the major pathway of intake, varies widely because of the age, sex, and diet of the organism. Diet is the major modifier of Pb absorption and of toxic effects in many species of domestic and laboratory animals, waterfowl, and aquatic organisms. In fact, the lack of certain major minerals in the diet often affected toxicity and storage of Pb in tissue more than did doubling the dosages of Pb in the diet (Levander 1979). Dietary deficiencies in calcium, zinc, iron, vitamin E, copper, thiamin, phosphorus, magnesium, fat, protein, minerals, and ascorbic acid increased Pb absorption and its toxic effects (Longcore et al. 1974b; Forbes and Sanderson 1978; Levander 1979; Sleet and Soares 1979; Colle et al. 1980; EPA 1980; Hodson et al. 1980; De Michele 1984; Stone and Fox 1984; Zmudzki et al. 1983, 1984; Carlson and Nielsen 1985; Gilmartin et al. 1985). Toxic effects of Pb-stressed fauna also were exacerbated when animals were fed diets containing excess cadmium, lactose, ethylenediaminetetraacetic acid, zinc, fat, protein, sodium citrate, ascorbate, amino acids, vitamin D, copper, mercury, fiber content, and nitrilotriacetic acid (Clemens et al. 1975; Forbes and Sanderson 1978; Nriagu 1978b; Levander 1979; EPA 1980; Krajnovic-Ozretic and Ozretic 1980; Burrows and Borchard 1982; Hamir et al. 1982; Zmudzki et al. 1983, 1984; De Michele 1984; Carlson and Nielson 1985). Protection against various toxic effects of ingested Pb was provided by measured dietary supplements of calcium, iron, zinc, ascorbic acid, and vitamin E (Krajnovic-Ozretic and Ozretic 1980; Gilmartin et al. 1985). Many other conditions affect Pb absorption, including size of Pb particle (EPA 1980; Hamir et al. 1982), type of Pb compound ingested (EPA 1980), presence of other compounds that act synergistically (Barth et al. 1973) or antagonistically (Luoma and Bryan 1978), and dosage (Finley and and Dieter 1978). For example, smaller Pb particles, <180 um in diameter, were absorbed from the intestinal tract up to 7 times more rapidly than larger particles of 180 to 250 um (EPA 1980). However, when large pieces of Pb are ingested, such as lead shot, these may lodge in the gastrointestinal tract, dissolve slowly, and cause Pb poisoning (Nriagu 1978b). Also, lead phthalates were absorbed more rapidly than carbonates, acetates, sulfides, and naphthanates, in that sequence (EPA 1980). It is evident that all of these variables, as well as diet, need to be considered in risk assessment of Pb.

BACKGROUND CONCENTRATIONS

GENERAL

Lead concentrations were usually highest in ecosystems nearest Pb mining, smelting, and refining activities; Pb storage battery recycling plants; areas of high vehicular traffic; urban and industrialized areas; sewage and spoil disposal areas; dredging sites; and areas of heavy hunting pressure. In general, Pb does not biomagnify in food chains. Older organisms usually contain the greatest body burdens, and Pb accumulations are greatest in bony tissues. It seems that resources that are now at high risk (i.e., increased mortality, reduced growth, or impaired reproduction) from Pb include the following: migratory waterfowl that congregate at heavily-hunted areas; raptors that eat hunter-wounded game; domestic livestock near smelters, refineries, and recycling plants; wildlife that forage extensively near heavily traveled roads; aquatic life in proximity to mining activities, Pb arsenate pesticides, metal finishing industries, lead alkyl production, and Pb aerosol fallout; and crops and invertebrates growing or living in Pb-contaminated soils. Data on background concentrations in nonbiological and living resources are cited extensively in Bernhard and Zattera (1975), Nriagu (1978a,b), Wong et al. (1978), Branica and Konrad (1980), Jenkins (1980), Eisler (1981), Harrison and Laxen (1981), and Demayo et al. (1982).

NONBIOLOGICAL SAMPLES

Average Pb concentrations in nonbiological materials worldwide were much higher in sediments (47,000 ug/kg), soils (16,000), and sediment interstitial waters (36) than in atmospheric and other hydrospheric compartments (Table 3). Most of the lead discharged into surface waters is rapidly incorporated into suspended and bottom sediments, and most will ultimately be found in marine sediments (Harrison and Laxen 1981). Sediments now constitute the largest global reservoir of Pb; sediment interstitial waters and soils constitute secondary reservoirs (Table 3).

Lead concentrations were elevated in certain nonbiological materials as a result of nonhunting human activities and natural processes (Table 4). In sediments, Pb concentrations ranged from 3 mg/kg in carbonate marls off the Florida coast to more than 11,000 mg/kg at Sorfjord, Norway, the site of massive discharges of Pb-containing industrial and domestic wastes (Nriagu 1978a). Lead contaminates sediments from sources as diverse as steelworks, shipyards, crude oil refineries, cement and ceramic factories, Pb storage battery recycling plants, and heavy traffic (Scoullos 1986). Mining activities are also important. High concentrations of Pb were measured in sediments (up to 2,200 mg/kg) and detritus (up to 7,000 mg/kg) of the Big River in southeastern Missouri (Czarneski 1985). The Big River drains what was once the largest Pb-mining district in the world; commercial mining was extensive between the early 1700's and 1972. During this period more than 200 metric tons of tailings accumulated within the Big River watershed as a result of seepage from tailings ponds, from erosion of tailings piles on the banks, and through accidental discharges (Niethammer et al. 1985).

Table 3. Amounts of lead in global reservoirs (modified from Nriagu 1978a).

Reservoir	Concentration (µg/kg)	Total Pb in pool (millions of metric tons)
Atmosphere	0.0035	0.018
Lithosphere		
Soils	16,000	4,800
Sediments	47,000	48,000,000
Hydrosphere		
Oceans	0.02	27.4
Sediment interstitial waters	36	12,000
Lakes and rivers	2	0.061
Glaciers	0.003	0.061
Groundwater	20	0.082
Biosphere		
Land biota		
Living	100	0.083
Dead	3,000	2.1
Marine biota		
Living	500	0.0008
Dead	2,500	2.5
Freshwater biota		
All	2,500	0.825

Table 4. Lead concentrations in selected nonbiological materials.

Material (units)	Concentration[a]	Reference[b]
Air (µg/m^3)		
Nonurban areas	0.1	EPA 1980
Urban areas	(0.3–2.5)	NRCC 1973
Metropolitan areas	(2–10)	EPA 1980
Rural roads	6	NRCC 1973
Heavy traffic	40	
Near industrial sources	May exceed 1,000	EPA 1980
Rain (µg/L		
Minnesota		
1979		
Rural	6	Eisenreich
Urban	29	et al. 1986

1983		
Rural	2	
Urban	4	
Atmospheric deposition (g/ha)		
New Jersey Pine Barrens		
1971–79	350	Turner et al. 1985
1980–82	140	
Ice (μg/L)		
Greenland		
800 BC	0.001	NRCC 1973
1750	0.01	
1940	0.07	
1973	>0.2	
Soils (mg/kg dry weight)		
Near Pb smelter		
Missouri	128	Burrows 1981
British Columbia	>1,000	
Distance from highway		
2 m	500	Krishnayya and
20 m	312	Bedi 1986
40 m	112	
60 m	46	
Near metal smelter	(1,200–2,700)	Beyer et al. 1985
Control site	(99–490)	
Near factory	(210–485)	Edwards and Clay 1977
Reference site (1,000 m distant)	(10–30)	
Worldwide	10 (2–200)	Demayo et al. 1982
USA	20 (10–700)	
Forest litter (g/ha)		
Vermont	20,000	Friedland and Johnson 1985
New Jersey	7,600	Turner et al. 1985
Water (μg/L)		
Egypt, Nile River		
Industrialized area	9.5	Fayed and Abd-El-Shafy 1985
Sweden		
Polluted lake		
Shallow water	3.3 (1.5–4.5)	Haux et al. 1986
Deep water	(8–41)	
Reference lake	0.1	
Greece, seawater		
Industrialized area	(2–5.5)	Scoullos 1986
USA		
Maine		

Pre-snowmobile	4.1	Adams 1975
Ice-out	135	
Nationwide		
Rivers	5 (0.6–120)	Demayo et al. 1982
Streams	23	
England		
Coastal sea water	Max. 2.3	
Offshore	(0.02–0.03)	
Solids entering		
surface waters (mg/kg dry weight)		
Street dust		
Urban	(1,000–4,000)	Harrison and
Rural	440	Laxen 1981
Highway runoff		
Suspended sediments	(3,100–5,800)	
Settleable solids	16,000	
Sewage sludge	(100–1,400)	
Suspended sediments		
in mineralized areas	(1,000–8,000)	
Integrated study (µg/kg		
Tennessee stream		
Water	(0.01–0.019)	Demayo et al. 1982
Dissolved solids	(30–84)	
Coarse particles	(124–653)	
Colloidal particles	(62–2,820)	
Sediments (mg/kg dry weight)		
Egypt, Nile River		
Industrialized area	Max. 1,800	Fayed and Abd-El-Shafy 1985
Greece		
Near major industries	(500–600)	Scoullos 1986
Several km distant	40	
Preindustrial levels	10	
Norway		
Sorfjord	Max. 11,000	Nriagu 1978a
Sweden		
Polluted lake	(2,000–2,500)	Haux et al. 1986
Reference lake	110	
USA		
Chesapeake Bay, 1979–81	(1–134)	Di Giulio and Scanlon 1985
Upper Mississippi River	13 (0.4–86)	Wiener et al. 1984
Southeastern Missouri,		
Big River, 1979–1981		
Sediments	(1,400–2,200)	Czarneski 1985

Organic detritus	(800–7,000)	
Florida	3	Nriagu 1978a
Oceanic		
Near shore	20	Demayo et al. 1982
Deep sea	45	
Clay	9	
Carbonate	80	

[a]Concentrations are shown as mean, minimum and maximum (in parentheses), and maximum (Max.).

[b]Each reference applies to data in the same row and in the rows that immediately follow for which no reference is indicated.

In soils, Pb concentrates in organic-rich surface horizons (NRCC 1973). In one instance, only 17 mg of soluble Pb/kg was found in soils 3 days after the addition of 2,784 mg of Pb (as lead nitrate)/kg (NRCC 1973). The estimated residence time of Pb in soils is about 20 years; complete turnover in topsoil is expected every few decades (Nriagu 1978a). In forest litter, however, the mean residence time of Pb is lengthy; estimates range from 220 years (Turner et al. 1985) to more than 500 years (Friedland and Johnson 1985).

Lead deposited on roadways is removed in drainage water, and later accumulated in roadside soils (Harrison et al. 1985). Amounts of Pb in roadside soils are increased as a direct result of the combustion of gasoline containing organolead additives. In general, the amounts of Pb were greatest along roads with the highest density of vehicular traffic, and amounts decreased rapidly with increasing distance from the roadway (Harrison and Dyer 1974; Boggess 1977; Chmiel and Harrison 1981; Way and Schroder 1982; Table 4). Elevated levels of Pb in soils also were recorded from the vicinity of storage battery reclamation plants, smelting activities, and mining and milling operations (Boggess 1977; Burrows 1981; Kisseberth et al. 1984). Fly ash from coal burned in homes or privately hauled from power plants, which contains 100 to 450 mg Pb/kg and is frequently used to reclaim land for the growth of forage and pasture crops and as an alkaline amendment in the reclamation of strip mined areas (Nriagu 1978a), is considered another source of soil Pb. Two additional sources of Pb in soils are municipal sewage sludge and lead-arsenate pesticides (Nriagu 1978a). Sewage sludge, which contains up to 100 mg Pb/kg and is applied as a fertilizer and soil conditioner at the rate of 50 million tons annually, may increase top soil levels by as much as 25 mg Pb/kg. Lead arsenate, a pesticide used to reduce bird hazards near airport runways by controlling earthworm abundance, and also to control pests in fruit orchards, represents another local source of lead contamination to soils.

Lead reaches the aquatic environment through industrial and municipal discharges, in atmospheric deposition, from weathering processes in areas of natural Pb mineralization, and in highway runoff (EPA 1980; Harrison and Laxen 1981; Birdsall et al. 1986). Industrial Pb input to aquatic environments is estimated at 10X that introduced by natural weathering processes (Scoullos 1986); sewage and aerosols are major sources (Harrison and Laxen 1981). Snowmobile exhausts are considered a major source of lead in some locations; concentrations up to 135 ug Pb/l have been recorded in surface waters at the time of ice breakup (Adams 1975). On the other hand, Pb content in water (and sediments) of a fly ash settling pond of a coal-fired power plant did not increase as a result of plant operations (White et al. 1986).

Anthropogenic activities leading to increased air Pb levels include primary and secondary lead smelting, the burning of gasoline containing lead antiknock agents, coal combustion, storage battery manufacture, and pigment production (NRCC 1973). It is generally agreed that combustion of leaded gasoline is the primary source of atmospheric Pb. Atmospheric Pb is usually attached to aerosols <0.2 um in diameter, is efficiently scavenged by precipitation, has a short atmospheric residence time that is usually measured in days but may range up to 14 weeks depending on meteorological conditions, and may be transported long distances (i.e., hundreds or thousands of kilometers) from emitting sources (NRCC 1973; Harrison and Laxen 1981; Harrison et al. 1985; Eisenreich et al. 1986). Along roadways, more than 90% of Pb emissions are dispersed by the atmosphere away from the immediate vicinity of the road; air Pb levels stabilize at low levels about 30 m from the road as a result of rapid settling of particles >5 um in diameter, and from the downwind traverse of particles entrained in the turbulent atmosphere (Boggess 1977; Harrison et al 1985). Since 1970, the lead content in

16

gasoline has decreased; profiles of Pb in dated sediment cores and Pb in atmospheric aerosols suggest that the environment is responding to decreasing use of leaded gasoline, and that atmospheric Pb concentrations and fluxes will continue to decrease susbstantially if use of Pb in gasoline is further decreased (Eisenreich et al. 1986).

FUNGI, MOSSES, LICHENS

Concentrations of Pb were highest in specimens collected near metal smelters, lead mines, industrial areas, and urban locations (Table 5). Lead concentrations were 9 to 13X greater in a lichen (*Parmelia baltimorensis*) collected in Washington, DC, in 1970 than in the same lichen collected 34 years earlier (Jenkins 1980).

TERRESTRIAL PLANTS

Elevated Pb contents were recorded in various species of plants from the vicinity of metal smelters, roadsides, soils heavily contaminated with Pb, natural ore deposits, and Pb recycling factories (Table 5). Bioavailability of Pb in soils to plants is limited, but is enhanced by reduced soil pH, reduced content of organic matter and inorganic colloids, reduced iron oxide and phosphorus content, and increased amounts of Pb in soils (NRCC 1973; Boggess 1977). Lead, when available, becomes associated with plants by way of active transport through roots and by absorption of Pb that adheres to foliage (Boggess 1977). Lead concentrations were always higher in the older parts of plants than in shoots or flowers (Bunzl and Kracke 1984; Table 5).

Table 5. Lead concentrations in field collections of selected species of flora and fauna. Values shown are in mg Pb/kg (ppm) fresh weight (FW), or dry weight (DW).

Taxonomic group, organism, tissue, and other variables	Concentration[a]	Reference[b]
Fungi, Mosses, and Lichens		
Fungi, 4 species		
Near metal smelter	4 DW	Beyer et al. 1985
Control site	2 DW	
Moss, *Brachythecium rivulare*		
Near lead mines	(1,330–8,206) DW	McLean and Jones 1975
Moss, *Hypnum cupressiforme*		
Sweden, museum specimens		
Year of collection		
1860	(18–27)DW	Ruhling and
1880	(20–37) DW	Tyler 1968
1900	(40–70) DW	
1920	(22–90) DW	
1940	(15–70) DW	
1960	(65–75) DW	
1968	(70–90) DW	
Vicinity urban industry	Max. 11,611 DW	Goodman and Roberts 1971
Lichen, *Parmelia baltimorensis*		
Washington, DC		
1938	106 DW	Jenkins 1980
1958	270 DW	
1970	(950–1,371) DW	

Connecticut, 1971	198 DW	
Algae and Macrophytes		
Acorns and berries, 4 species		
Near metal smelter	4 DW	Beyer et al. 1985
Control site	3 DW	
Aquatic macrophytes, whole		
Nile River, Egypt		
Industrialized area	Max. 22 DW	Fayed and
Abd-El-Shafy 1985		
Aquatic plants, 7 species		
From lead shot seeded area		
Roots	19 DW	Behan et al. 1979
Shoots	3 DW	
Control area		
Roots	5 DW	
Shoots	1 DW	
Swiss chard, *Beta vulgaris cicla*		
Leaf		
15 m from highway	220 DW	Jenkins 1980
20 m from highway	154 DW	
Control area	<3 DW	
Alga, *Blidingia minima*		
Whole, Raritan Bay, New Jersey		
Water Pb content		
0.002 mg/L	12 DW	Seeliger and
0.01 mg/L	172 DW	Edwards 1977
Brome grass, *Bromus* spp.		
Grown in soil with 680 mg Pb/kg	34 DW	Jenkins 1980
Control	7 DW	
Weed, *Cassia* sp., India		
Distance from highway (meters)		
2	(208–303) DW	Krishnayya and
20	(90–97) DW	Bedi 1986
40	(55–68) DW	
60	(20–22) DW	
Green alga, *Cladophora* sp.		
Missouri, tailings pond	11,300 DW	
1.6–4.0 km downstream	(200–4,600) DW	
6.1–9.6 km downstream	(100–2,600) DW	
Alga, *Enteromorpha llinza*		
Whole, Raritan Bay, New Jersey		
Water Pb content		
0.002 mg/L	18 DW	Seeliger and

0.01 mg/L	68 DW	Edwards 1977
Red fescue grass, *Festuca rubra*		
Leaf, Wales, UK		
Distance downwind from smelter		
1.5 km	814 DW	Goodman and
8 km	30 DW	Roberts 1971
25 km	14 DW	
>25 km	(5–12) DW	
Foliage, 8 species		
Near metal smelter	21 DW	Beyer et al. 1985
Control site	10 DW	
Alga, *Fucus distichus*		
Distance from Pb deposit		
1 km	1 DW	Bohn 1979
2 km	0.6 DW	
Alga, *Fucus vesiculosus*		
Whole, Raritan Bay, New Jersey		
Water Pb content		
0.002 mg/L	8 DW	Seeliger and
0.01 mg/L	38 DW	Edwards 1977
Lettuce, *Lactuca satvia*		
Pb-contaminated areas	71 FW	Demayo et al. 1982
Uncontaminated areas	0.5 FW	
Mule deer forage, Colorado,		
Roadside		
1978	59 DW	Harrison and
1979	42 DW	Dyer 1984
Rice, *Oryza sativa*		
Grown 10 m from highway		
Grain	0.2 DW	Ter Haar 1970
Straw	5.8 DW	
Grown 230 m from highway		
Grain	0.2 DW	
Straw	2.1 DW	
Spruce, *Picea abies*, Germany, 1984		
Declining spruce forest		
Litter	416 DW	Backhaus and
Needles	13 DW	Backhaus 1986
Nondeclining stand		
Litter	213 DW	
Needles	2 DW	
Shortleaf pine, *Pinus echinata*		
Missouri, leaf		

Distance from smelter, km		
0.8	3,546 (420–11,750) DW	Bolter et al. 1973
0.8–1.6	497 (101–1,475) DW	
1.6–2.4	274 (52–1,050) DW	
2.4–3.2	142 (62–412) DW	
3.2	123 (22–661) DW	
Pondweed, *Potamogeton* sp.		
Missouri, tailings pond	11,300 DW	Jenkins 1980
1.6 km downstream	3,500 DW	
8.1 km downstream	100 DW	
Black cherry, *Prunus serotina*		
Leaves, 1978		
Near roadway	(9–14) DW	Beyer and Moore 1980
>30 m distant	(2–6) DW	
Potato, *Solanum tuberosum*		
Pb-contaminated areas	13 FW	Demayo et al. 1982
Uncontaminated areas	1 FW	
Submerged aquatic vegetation, 1979–81		
Chesapeake Bay, 5 species	7.4 (0.5–30) DW	Di Giulio and Scanlon 1985
Alga, *Ulva* sp.		
Whole, Raritan Bay, New Jersey		
Water Pb content		
0.002 mg/L	20 DW	Seeliger and
0.01 mg/L	76 DW	Edwards 1977
Blueberry, *Vaccinium pallidum*		
Leaf, Missouri		
Distance from smelter		
1.6–3.2 km	495 (141–874) DW	Jenkins 1980
3.2–4.8 km	203 DW	
4.8–6.5 km	76 DW	
6.5–8.1 km	68 DW	
8.1–9.7 km	64 DW	
9.7–11.3 km	41 (29–101) DW	
Vegetation		
Vermont forest		
Root bark	33 DW	Friedland and
Twigs	28 DW	Johnson 1985
Bark	23 DW	
Root wood	10 DW	
Foliage	3 DW	
Wood	3 DW	
New Jersey Pine Barrens		

Roots	18 DW	Turner et al. 1985
Bark	15 DW	
Foliage	4 DW	
Wood	0.5 DW	
Near roadway, UK 1979		
Grass	63 DW	Chmiel and
Grass seeds	99 DW	Harrsion 1981
Hawthorn, *Crataegus* spp.		
Leaves	146 DW	
Fruit	4 DW	
Control site, UK 1979		
Grass	2 DW	
Grass seeds	4 DW	
Hawthorn		
Leaves	4 DW	
Fruit	2 DW	
Grass		
Near factory	(830–1,840) DW	Edwards and
1,000 m distant		Clay 1977
Growing	(120–1,200) DW	
Dead and litter	(370–1,570) DW	
1,700 m distant		
Growing	(240–420) DW	
Dead and litter	(170–1,970) DW	
Near Pb smelter, forage		
Missouri	979 FW	Burrows 1981
British Columbia	(100–200) FW	
Kansas, vegetation		
Near highway	11 DW	Robel et al. 1981
Distant site	3 DW	
Invertebrates		
Limpet, *Acmaea digitalis*		
California		
Near bridges		
Soft parts	931 DW	Graham 1972
Shell	108 DW	
Pb-free area		
Soft parts	8 DW	
Shell	9 DW	
Bee, *Apis* sp.		
Honey		
Pb-contaminated area	(1–8) FW	Demayo et al. 1982
Uncontaminated area	<0.5 FW	

Sea urchin, *Arbacia lixula*		
Soft parts, Italy		
Unpolluted	21 DW	Sheppard and
Polluted	58 DW	Bellamy 1974
Beetles, *Coleoptera*, UK 1979		
Near roadway	32 DW	Chmiel and
Control site	1 DW	Harrison 1981
Bivalve molluscs, 3 species, soft parts, Chesapeake Bay, 1979–81	5 (0.6–27) DW	Di Giulio and
Scanlon 1985		
Crawfish, *Cambarus* sp.		
Whole, Missouri		
At tailings pond	500 DW	Gale et al. 1976
1 km downstream	400 DW	
25 km downstream	2 DW	
Dung beetles, whole		
Near roadway	13 DW	Robel et al. 1981
Distant site	6 DW	
Earthworms, whole		
Blacksburg, VA, 1974		
From high traffic density		
area (21,000 vehicles/day)		
6 m from highway	51 DW	Goldsmith and
18 m distant	32 DW	Scanlon 1977
From low traffic density area		
(1,100 vehicles/day)		
18 m distant	12 DW	
Near highway	(38–331) DW	Beyer and Moore 1980
Earthworm, *Eisenia rosea*		
Whole, Illinois		
Control areas	32 DW	Jenkins 1980
From areas receiving sludge		
at 1600 kg Pb/hectare	624 DW; Max. 981 DW	
Earthworm, *Eisenoides carolinensis*		
Whole, uncontaminated area	2,100 DW	Beyer and Cromartie 1987
Insects, various species		
Distance from highway		
0–7 meters		
Sucking	16 DW	Anderson 1977
Chewing	27 DW	
Predatory	31 DW	
13–20 meters		
Sucking	9 DW	

Chewing	10 DW	
Predatory	20 DW	
>20 meters		
Sucking	5 DW	
Chewing	5 DW	
Predatory	6 DW	
Kansas, 1978		
Near roadway	50 DW	Udevitz et al. 1980
Control site	15 DW	
Lepidopteran larvae, UK, 1979		
Near roadway	118 DW	Chmiel and
Control site	<1 DW	Harrison 1981
Earthworm, *Lumbricus terrestris*		
Whole, Maryland		
Distance from highway, meters		
3.0	269 DW	Gish and
6.1	113 DW	Christensen 1973
12.2	80 DW	
24.4	43 DW	
48.8	52 DW	
Eastern tent caterpillar, *Malacosoma americanum*		
Whole, 1978		
Near roadway	7 DW	Beyer and Moore 1980
>10 m distant	<5.3 DW	
Millipedes, Diplopoda		
UK 1979		
Near roadway	162 DW	Chmiel and
Control site	34 DW	Harrison 1981
USA		
Near highway	(43–82) DW	Beyer and Moore 1980
Coral, *Montastrea annularis*		
Virgin Islands, 1980, skeleton		
Polluted reef (Sewage, dredging)	0.4 FW	Dodge and
Pristine reef	0.09 FW	Gilbert 1984
Blue mussel, *Mytilus edulis*		
Soft parts		
Germany	(2–6) DW	Jenkins 1980
New Zealand	12 (<3–25) DW	
Norway	(2–3,100) DW	
England	9 DW; (0.5–3) FW	
Australia	(0.7–10) FW	
Spain	(2–15) DW	
Greenland	(2–21) FW	

Beetle, *Nicrophorus tomentosus* whole

Near metal smelter	3 DW	Beyer et al. 1985
Control site	2 DW	

Grass shrimp, *Palaemonetes pugio*

Whole, Virginia

Natural marsh	0.2 DW	Drifmeyer and
Spoil disposal area	11 DW	Odum 1975

Shrimp, *Pandalus montagui*

Soft parts

Sewage dump area	31 DW	Mackay et al. 1972
Control area	24 DW	

Sea urchin, *Paracentrotus lividus*

Soft parts, Italy

Unpolluted	20 DW	Sheppard and
Polluted	42 DW	Bellamy 1974

Caterpillar, *Porethetria dispar* Whole

Near metal smelter	9 DW	Beyer et al. 1985
Control site	3 DW	

Blackfly, *Simulium* sp.

Larva

Missouri

Tailings pond	14,233 DW	Gale et al. 1976
Illinois	24 DW	Anderson 1977

Slugs, Gastropoda, UK, 1979

Near roadway	141 DW	Chmiel and
Control site	27 DW	Harrison 1981

Spiders, Aranea, UK, 1979

Near roadway	560 DW	
Control site	<1 DW	

Tubificid worms

Rural streams	16 DW	Boggess 1977
Urban streams	367 DW	

Woodlice, Isopoda

UK, 1979

Near roadway	152 DW	Chmiel and
Control site	19 DW	Harrison 1981

USA

Near highway	(380–682) DW	Beyer and Moore 1980

Fish

Spotted wolffish, *Anarhichas minor*

Near Pb mine, Greenland

Liver	Max. 1.8 FW	Bollingberg and
Muscle	Max. 0.12 FW	Johansen 1979

Coastal marine fishes, USA

  Liver

5 species	(<0.1–0.2) FW	Hall et al. 1978
20 species	(0.2–0.4) FW	
33 species	(0.4–0.6) FW	
13 species	(0.6–0.8) FW	
6 species	(0.8–1) FW	
5 species	(1–3) FW	

  Muscle

5 species	(0.1–0.3) FW
92 species	(0.3–0.5) FW
51 species	(0.5–0.7) FW
7 species	(0.7–1) FW
4 species	(1–3) FW

Whitefish, *Coregonus* spp., Sweden

Liver

Polluted lake	(6–7) DW	Haux et al. 1986
Reference lake	<1 DW	

Fish

  Upper Mississippi River
  (Minnesota-Iowa), 1979

  Common carp, *Cyprinus carpio*

Whole	3(1–12) DW	Wiener et al. 1984
Liver	9 (2–32) DW	

  Bluegill, *Lepomis macrochirus*

Whole	0.4 (0.2–1.1) DW

Fish, whole

  Nationwide

1971	Max. 1.4 FW	Walsh et al. 1977
1972	0.4 (Max. 5.2) FW	
1973	Max. 1.4 FW	
1976–77	0.3 FW	May and McKinney 1981
1978–79	0.2 (0.1–6.7) FW	Lowe et al. 1984
1980–81	0.2 (0.1–1.9) FW	

  Southeastern Missouri, Big River

  Upstream from mine site

Catostomids, 3 species	<0.1 FW	Schmitt et al. 1984
Other species	<0.3 FW	

  Downstream

Catostomids	0.4–0.8 FW
Longear sunfish, *Lepomis megalotis*	18 FW
Black redhorse, *Moxostoma duquesnei*	15 FW
Smallmouth bass, *Micropterus dolomieui*	9 FW

Bluegill, whole
Missouri, mine tailings pond,

At pond	128 DW	Gale et al. 1976
1 km downstream	23 DW	
65 km downstream	5 DW	

Plaice, *Platichthys flesus*, whole
Polluted area, UK

Age 2+	20 DW	Hardisty et al. 1974
Age 3+	24 DW	
Age 4+	26 DW	
Age 5+	28 DW	

Uncontaminated area, UK

Age 2+	14 DW
Age 3+	16 DW
Age 4+	18 DW
Age 5+	19 DW

Integrated studies
Great Lakes, Lake Ontario

Plankton	4 DW	Demayo et al. 1982
Zooplankton	(1–5) DW	
Fish	(0.1–0.13) FW	

Marine food chain, Central Pacific

Seawater	0.006 FW	Flegal 1985
Phytoplankton	0.05 FW	
Zooplankton	0.04 FW	
Carnivores, muscle		
Intermediate (anchovy)	0.02 FW	
Top (tuna)	0.0003 FW	

Oklahoma pond

Water	0.013 FW	Demayo et al. 1982
Sediments		
Surface	529 DW	
12 cm depth	206 DW	
Plantkton	281 DW	
Benthos	37 DW	
Mosquitofish, *Gambusia* sp.	11 DW	

Amphibians and reptiles
Amphibians, whole

Near metal smelter	No species found	Beyer et al. 1985
Control site, 5 species	12 DW	

Frog, *Rana* sp., tadpole, whole

Missouri, tailings pond	4,139 DW	Gale et al. 1976
Distance downstream		

from tailings pond		
1 km	552 DW	
25 km	37 DW	
Southeastern Missouri, 1981–82, Big River		
Bullfrog, *Rana catesbeiana*, carcass		
Upstream from mine site	1 (Max. 6) FW	Niethammer et al.
Downstream	33 (Max. 300) FW	1985
Northern water snake, *Nerodia sipedon*, carcass		
Upstream	0.2 (Max. 0.6) FW	
Downstream	7 (Max. 14) FW	
Common box turtle, *Terrapene carolina* (Age 15 years)		
Near lead smelter, Missouri		
Humerus	51 FW	Beresford et al.
Femur	64 FW	1981
Liver	21 FW	
Kidney	24 FW	
Blood	6 FW	
Skin	0.4 FW	
Near Morgantown WV, Control site (Age 17 years)		
Humerus	4 FW	
Femur	4 FW	
Liver	1 FW	
Kidney	2 FW	
Blood	0.1 FW	
Skin	0.1 FW	
Toad, *Xenopus laevis*		
Fed worms from Pb-contaminated soils		
Bone	24 FW	Ireland 1977
Skin	3 FW	
Muscle	1 FW	
Kidney	15 FW	
Liver	7 FW	
Fed uncontaminated worms		
Bone	5 FW	
Skin	0.8 FW	
Muscle	0.6 FW	
Kidney	3 FW	
Liver	1 FW	

Birds

Canvasback, *Aythya valisineria*
  Blood
    Chesapeake Bay, 1974
      Normal   (0.059–0.064) FW   Dieter et al. 1976
      Abnormal (17%)   0.263 FW
  Wingbone
    La Crosse, Wisconsin
    1976
      Males   18 (6–56) DW   Fleming 1981
      Females   5 (1–20) DW
      Immatures
        Males   0.8 (0.1–4) DW
        Females   1 (0–21) DW
    1977
      Males   11 (9–12) DW
      Females   8 (1–48) DW
      Immatures
        Males   0.8 (<0.1–7) DW
        Females   <0.5 DW
    Keokuk, Iowa
    1976
      Males   6 (4–10) DW
      Females   5 (1–20) DW
      Immatures
        Males   0.5 (0.1–2) DW
        Females   1 (0.1–22) DW
    1977
      Males   2 (0.2–19) DW
      Females   4 (1–19) DW
Birds
  Galveston Bay, Texas,
  1980–81, 3 species, liver   (0.1–0.5) FW   King and Cromartie 1986
  Texas
    Probers with Pb shot in gizzards
      Bone   11 FW   Hall and Fisher 1985
      Feather   4 FW
      Liver   0.3 FW
    Probers without Pb shot in gizzards
      Bone   6 FW
      Feather   5 FW
      Liver   <0.1 FW
    Non-probers
      Bone   6 FW

Feather	2 FW	
Liver	<0.1 FW	
Ruffed grouse, *Bonasa umbellus*		
Virginia, rural areas		
Liver	2.3 DW	Kendall et al. 1984
Bone	2.8 (0.4–9) DW	
Knot, *Calidris canutus*		
Feather		
Juvenile	2 DW	Goede and
Adult	7 DW	de Voogt 1985
Rock dove, *Columba livia*		
UK		
Urban area		
Kidney		
Female	204 DW; (9–30) FW	Johnson et al. 1982
Male	122 DW	
Bone		
Female	338 DW	
Male	126 DW	
Rural area		
Kidney		
Female	6 DW; (1.2–1.9) FW	
Male	8 DW	
Bone		
Female	16 DW	
Male	19 DW	
Tokyo, Japan		
Femur		
Urban areas	(16–31) FW	Ohi et al. 1974
Suburban areas	(2–3) FW	
Kidney		
Urban areas	(2–3) FW	
Suburban areas	<1 FW	
Mute swan, *Cygnus olor*		
Denmark, 1982		
Blood		
Adults	0.25 (0.13–0.54) FW	Eskildsen and Grandjean 1984
Juveniles	0.11 (0.07–0.39) FW	
Peregrine falcon, *Falco peregrinus*		
Baltimore, Maryland, Age 7+		
Liver	0.8 FW	De Ment et al. 1986
Kidney	1.4 FW	
Prey organism		

Rock dove

Urban

    Blood   1 (0.3–17) FW

    Liver   3 FW

    Kidney   9 FW

    Whole   5 FW

Rural

    Blood   <0.1 FW

    Liver   0.4 FW

    Kidney   0.5 FW

    Whole   0.3 FW

Common loon, *Gavia immer*, Pb poisoned

Liver   (21–39) FW   Locke et al. 1982

Bald eagle, *Haliaeetus leucocephalus*

  Nationwide, 1978–81, found dead,

  suspected Pb poisoning

    Liver   28 (11–61) FW   Reichel et al. 1984

    Liver

      Control   0.6 FW   Bagley and Locke 1967

      Pb-poisoned   21 FW   Mulhern et al. 1970

Barn swallow, *Hirundo rustica*

Near Baltimore-Washington Parkway, 1979

Feather

    Male   67 (55–82) DW   Grue et al. 1984

    Female   54 (43–68) DW

    Nestling   2 (2–3) DW

Carcass

    Male   5 (4–6) DW

    Female   9 (6–12) DW

    Nestling   2 (1–2) DW

Stomach contents

    Male   5 DW

    Female   7 DW

    Nestling   3 DW

Reference colony, 1979

  Feather

    Male   24 (21–28) DW

    Female   19 (16–22) DW

    Nestling   2 (2–3) DW

  Carcass

    Male   4 (3–5) DW

    Female   5 (3–7) DW

    Nestling   1 DW

Stomach contents
  Male   0.2 DW
  Female   2 DW
  Nestling   2 DW

House sparrow, *Passer domesticus*

Illinois

  Urban areas

Feather	158 DW	Getz et al. 1977a
Intestine	26 DW	
Liver	12 DW	
Lung	7 DW	
Kidney	34 DW	
Femur	130 DW	
Muscle	2 DW	

  Rural areas

Feather	27 DW
Intestine	2 DW
Liver	0.6 DW
Lung	0.9 DW
Kidney	3 DW
Femur	17 DW
Muscle	0.9 DW

Brown pelican, *Pelecanus occidentalis*

Egg

South Carolina 1971–72	0.03 (0.01–0.11) FW	Blus et al. 1977
Florida, 1969–70	0.03 (0.01–0.05) FW	

Liver

  Found dead

  1972

Georgia	0.1 FW
Florida	0.1 FW

  1973

South Carolina	0.3 FW
Florida	0.2 FW

  Shot, 1970

Florida	0.1 FW
South Carolina	0.1 FW

Sora rail, *Porzana carolina*

Maryland

Lead shot in gizzard

Liver	(0.1–17) FW	Stendell et al. 1980
Bone	(1–127) DW	

No lead shot in gizzard

Liver	(<0.01–0.08) FW	
Bone	(<0.4–42) DW	
Songbirds, carcass		
Near metal smelter, 10 species	56 (9–240) DW	Beyer et al. 1985
Control site, 9 species	15 (6–25) DW	
Southeastern Missouri,		
1981–82, Big River		
Green backed heron, *Butorides striatus*		
Liver		
Upstream from mine site	0.1 (Max. 0.3 FW	Niethammer
Downstream	0.5 (Max. 1.5) FW	et al. 1985
Northern rough–winged swallow, *Stelgidopteryx serripennis*		
Carcass		
Upstream from mine site	0.5 (Max. 5) FW	
Downstream	1 (Max. 15) FW	
European starling, *Sturnus vulgaris*		
Nesting near highway, Maryland		
Carcass	(4–10) DW	Grue et al. 1986
Feathers	(7–52) DW	
Stomach contents	(84–94) DW	
Control site		
Carcass	(1–3) DW	
Feathers	(3–14) DW	
Stomach contents	(6–7) DW	
Nationwide, whole less beaks, skins, wings and feet		
1971	1.3 (0.1–6.6) FW	Martin and
Chicago, Ill.	5.0 FW	Nickerson 1973
Indiana, urban	3.4 FW	
Quincy, MA	6.6 FW	
Jamestown, NY	5.1 FW	
1973	0.9 (<0.1–3.2) FW	White et al. 1977
Urban	1.1 (<0.1–3.2) FW	
Rural	0.7 (<0.1–2.4) FW	
Robin, *Turdus migratorius*		
Illinois		
Urban areas		
Feather	79 DW	Getz et al. 1977a
Intestine	24 DW	
Liver	10 DW	
Lung	10 DW	
Kidney	25 DW	
Femur	133 DW	
Muscle	1 DW	

Rural areas		
Feather	25 DW	
Intestine	3 DW	
Liver	2 DW	
Lung	2 DW	
Kidney	7 DW	
Femur	41 DW	
Muscle	1 DW	
Waterfowl, nationwide, 7 species		
Wingbones, 1972–73	(<0.5–361) DW	Stendell et al. 1979
Mallard, *Anas platyrhynchos*		
Adult	12 DW	
Immature	10 DW	
Pacific flyaway		
Alaska	6 DW	
Washington		
Eastern	8 DW	
Western	24 DW	
Oregon		
Columbia River	45 DW	
Other	15 DW	
California		
Merced	15 DW	
Sacramento	38 DW	
Other	25 DW	
Northern pintail, *Anas acuta*		
Adult	7 DW	
Immature	6 DW	
Mottled duck, *Anas fulvigula*		
Adult	48 DW	
Immature	40 DW	
Canvasback		
Adult	17 DW	
Immature	8 DW	
Redhead, *Aythya americana*		
Adult	26 DW	
Immature	24 DW	
Lesser scaup, *Aythya affinis*		
Adult	3 DW	
Immature	2 DW	
Black duck, *Anas rubripes*		
Adult	8 DW	

Mammals

Field mouse, *Apodemus sylvaticus*
Near abandoned Pb mine

Whole body	(9–14) DW	Roberts et al. 1978
Kidney	(39–46) DW	
Liver	(12–13) DW	
Bone	(189–352) DW	
Brain	(6–13) DW	
Muscle	(7–10) DW	

Control area

Whole body	1 DW
Kidney	(9–13) DW
Liver	(5–8) DW
Bone	(11–21) DW
Brain	(3–4) DW
Muscle	(5–6) DW

Short-tailed shrew, *Blarina brevicauda*
Carcass

Near metal smelter	109 DW	Beyer et al. 1985
Control site	18 DW	

From area of high traffic levels
(>12,000 vehicles/day)

Total body	18 DW	Getz et al. 1977c
Gut	24 DW	
Spleen	4 DW	
Liver	5 DW	
Lung	17 DW	
Kidney	12 DW	
Femur	67 DW	
Muscle	10 DW	

From area of low traffic levels
(<400 vehicles/day)

Total body	6 DW
Gut	3 DW
Spleen	2 DW
Liver	1 DW
Lung	8 DW
Kidney	4 DW
Femur	12 DW
Muscle	5 DW

Cow, *Bos bovis*
Missouri, hair
Near Pb smelter

Fall	94 DW	Dorn et al. 1974

Winter	87 DW	
Spring	96 DW	
Summer	66 DW	
Control area		
Fall	2 DW	
Winter	4 DW	
Spring	2 DW	
Summer	1 DW	
Dung		
Near roadway	10 DW	Robel et al. 1981
Distant site	8 DW	
Dog, *Canis familiaris*		
Blood		
Healthy	(0.01–0.05) FW	NRCC 1973
Pb-poisoned	(0.06–0.15) FW	
Big brown bat, *Eptesicus fuscus*		
Whole, minus GI tract and large embryos		
Males47 (20–90) FW	Clark 1979	
Females	32 (20–56) FW	
Guano	61 DW	
Stomach contents	4 DW	
Horse, *Equus caballus*		
Near smelter, British Columbia		
Liver	18 FW	Burrows 1981
Kidney	16 FW	
Bone	88 FW	
Near Pb smelter (some deaths), California		
Liver	(15–222) FW	Knight and
Kidney	(14–80) FW	Burau 1973
Blood (0.4–0.5) FW		
Control areas		
Blood	(0.1–0.3) FW	Jenkins 1980
Bank vole, *Clethrionomys glareolus*		
Whole body		
Near abandoned Pb mine	(16–21) DW	Roberts et al. 1978
Control area	(2–3) DW	
Chipmunk, *Eutamias townsendii*		
Hair		
Roadside location	235 DW	Raymond and
Control area	6 DW	Forbes 1975
Prairie vole, *Microtus ochrogaster*		
Illinois, whole body		

Near heavy traffic	8 DW	Getz et al. 1977b
Control area	3 DW	
Little brown bat, *Myotis lucifugus*		
Whole	17 (11–29) FW	Clark 1979
Guano	65 DW	
Stomach contents	26 FW	
Bats, *Myotis* spp., Florida 1981–83		
Guano	(3–6) DW	Clark et al. 1986
White-tailed deer, *Odocoileus virginianus*		
Near zinc smelter, Pennsylvania		
Feces	16 (6–37) DW	Sileo and Beyer 1985
Bone	9 (4–17) DW	
Teeth	6 (3–11) DW	
Kidney	2 (1–3) DW	
Liver	<2 DW	
Control area, 100 km from smelter		
Feces	8 (4–16) DW	
Bone	6 (3–11) DW	
Teeth	2 (1–4) DW	
Kidney	0.8 (0.5–1) DW	
Liver	<0.4 DW	
Muskrat, *Ondatra zibethicus*		
Liver		
Upstream from mine site	0.2 (Max. 0.3) FW	Niethammer
Downstream	0.7 (Max. 1.6) FW	et al. 1985
Sheep, *Ovis aries*		
Meat	<0.2 FW	Bunzl and
Liver	<1.5 FW	Kracke 1984
Kidney	<1.1 FW	
Sheep forage		
Grass		
Green	<12 FW	
Old	<33 FW	
Other	<24 FW	
White-footed mouse, *Peromyscus leucopus*		
Carcass		
Near metal smelter	17 DW	Beyer et al. 1985
Control site	7 DW	
Deer mice, *Peromyscus maniculatus*		
From high bone density traffic area		
Bone	52 DW	Mierau and
Kidney	9 DW	Favara 1975
Liver	3 DW	

Brain	1 DW	
Feces	154 DW	
From low density traffic area		
Bone	5 DW	
Kidney	3 DW	
Liver	1 DW	
Brain	0.1 DW	
Feces	7 DW	
Roadside locations		
Brain	(0.6–0.8) DW	Jenkins 1980
Liver	(0.9–3) DW	
Kidney	(2–8) DW	
Bone	(14–52) DW	
Hair	235 DW	
Control areas		
Brain	0.1 DW	
Liver	1 DW	
Kidney	3 DW	
Bone	5 DW	
Hair	6 DW	
Illinois, 1982		
Distance from lead battery reclamation plant		
100 m		
Liver	4 FW	Kisseberth
Kidney	13 FW	et al. 1984
Bone	79 FW	
1,000 m		
Liver	1 FW	
Kidney	3 FW	
Bone	2 FW	
Whole, 1978–79		
Near Cu-Zn mine		
Juveniles	4 FW	Smith and
Adults	5 FW	Rongstad 1982
Control site		
Juveniles	0.5 FW	
Adults	0.7 FW	
Raccoon, *Procyon lotor*		
Connecticut, Pb-intoxicated		
Liver, kidney	>35 FW	Diters and Nielsen 1978
Commensal rat, *Rattus norvegicus*		
Houston, Texas, 1978–79		
Urban		

Bone	125 FW	Way and
Kidney	9 FW	Schroder 1982
Stomach contents	31 FW	
Feces	72 FW	
Rural		
Bone	8 FW	
Kidney	3 FW	
Stomach contents	3 FW	
Feces	8 FW	
Roadside mammals, 1976		
Whole, minus GI tract and large embryos		
Short-tailed shrew		
Near highway	26 (6–130) FW	Clark 1979
Distant site	2 FW	
Meadow vole, *Microtus pennsylvanicus*		
Near highway	2 (0.2–5) FW	
Distant site	<1.4 FW	
White-footed mouse		
Near highway	5 (0.4–41) FW	
Distant site	1 (0.3–13) FW	
Common shrew, *Sorex araneus*, UK, 1979		
Near roadway		
Liver	17 DW	Chmiel and
Kidney	46 DW	Harrison 1981
Bone	193 DW	
Pelt	10 DW	
Control site		
Liver	<1 DW	
Kidney	9 DW	
Bone	41 DW	
Pelt	3 DW	

aConcentrations are listed as mean, (minimum-maximum), and maximum (Max.).

bEach reference applies to data in the same row and in the rows that immediately follow for which no reference is indicated.

Damage to plants with elevated Pb contents is usually negligible, but varies widely among species. Atmospheric Pb may have contributed to the decline of European spruce forests. The mean Pb content of needles and litter was significantly higher where tree decline was most pronounced than in areas where forests were unaffected (Backhaus and Backhaus 1986). Lead can have deleterious effects on plant growth processes at current Pb levels in urban areas and may similarly affect plants in rural areas in the future (Rolfe and Reinbold 1977). A reduction in yield of corn or soybeans is expected in low-binding capacity soils with Pb levels greater than 200 mg/kg (Rolfe and Reinbold 1977). Hay grown near roadsides may be toxic to horses and cattle (Rolfe and Reinbold 1977). In extreme cases, reforestation has been initiated in areas where forage is so heavily contaminated with Pb that it has become necessary to slaughter domestic livestock because the amounts of Pb in their livers and kidneys became unacceptably high (Edwards and Clay 1977). Typical area reforestation includes removal of contaminated forage by cutting, bailing, and burying native grasses; burning of stubble and litter; and adding of agricultural lime at the rate of 2,244 kg/ha (2,000 pounds/acre) to all soils within 1,525 m (5,000 feet) of sites where Pb levels exceed 175 mg/kg (Edwards and Clay 1977).

TERRESTRIAL INVERTEBRATES

In earthworms, lead levels were highest in those closest to highways and in areas with high volumes of traffic (Goldsmith and Scanlon 1977; Table 5). Various species of insects and soil invertebrates from roadsides, from areas receiving sewage sludge, and from metal smelter environs also contain high amounts of Pb (Table 5). Amounts of Pb in whole body were higher in earthworms, millipedes, and woodlice collected from soil and plant litter near highways than away from highways; soil and litter seem to be major reservoirs of Pb in roadside communities (Malacosoma americanum) and their host plant (Beyer and Moore 1980). In contrast, Pb concentrations in the eastern tent caterpillar (Malacosoma americanum) were lower than those reported for roadside soil and litter invertebrates, and were about 76% of that in leaves of its host, the black cherry Prunus serotina (Beyer and Moore 1980).

The use of terrestrial invertebrates as sentinel organisms has been suggested for monitoring Pb. The spider Araneus umbricatus, for example, contained Pb body burdens that correlated with that in a lichen (Lecanora conizaeoides) that is currently used to monitor atmospheric Pb (Clausen 1984). Similarly, the woodlouse (Porcellio scaber) seems to reflect Pb concentrations in adjacent soil or leaf litter (Hopkin et al. 1986).

AQUATIC BIOTA

Freshwater algae, invertebrates, and fish had comparatively elevated Pb concentrations when collected near industrialized areas, ponds with high numbers of Pb shot, urban areas, Pb mines, and tailings ponds (Table 5). For marine biota, Pb residues were highest where Pb concentrations were high in the water--near bridges, near industrial disposal areas, near sewage and disposal areas, near dredging sites, and at mining sites (Table 5). Among aquatic biota, Pb concentrations were usually highest in algae and benthic organisms, and lowest in upper trophic level predators. No significant biomagnification of Pb occurs in aquatic food chains (Boggess 1977; Rolfe and Reinbold 1977; Branica and Konrad 1980; Demayo et al. 1982; Flegal 1985; Table 5). Lead concentrations in cartilaginous and bony fishes--and also birds and mammals--were usually highest in areas of high human and vehicular density, and near lead mines and ore concentration plants. Lead concentrations in aquatic (and terrestrial) vertebrates tend to increase with increasing age of the organism, and to localize in hard tissues such as bone and teeth (Eisler 1981, 1984).

In stream sediments, Pb was highest in urban streams and lowest in the rural streams, reflecting Pb inputs from storm runoff; species diversity was greater in the rural streams, due partly to lowered contaminant loadings, including Pb (Rolfe and Reinbold 1977).

Nationwide monitoring of freshwater fishes conducted periodically by the U.S. Fish and Wildlife Service (National Biocontaminant Monitoring Program) showed that whole body Pb burdens were highest for Atlantic coast streams, the Great Lakes drainage, the Mississippi River system, the Columbia River system, and in certain Hawaiian streams (May and McKinney 1981). Major sources of Pb in Atlantic coast streams included wastes from metal finishing industries, brass manufacturing, lead alkyl production, primary and secondary Pb smelting, coal combustion, and manufacture of lead oxide. For the Great Lakes, especially for the Lake St. Clair collection site, industrial sources and urban Pb aerosol fallout from the Detroit area were major sources. In the Mississippi River system, naturally occurring deposits of Pb ores, and effluents from zinc producers and industrial dischargers were prevalent. The Columbia River system was characterized by Pb inputs from natural geologic deposits, industrial effluents, and the mining and smelting of Pb. Hawaiian streams received most of their Pb from urban runoff, vehicle sources, and agricultural and residential use of Pb arsenate (May and McKinney 1981).

Fish collected in 1979-1981 in the Big River, Missouri, near a ruptured tailings pond dam where Pb concentrations in tailings approached 4,000 mg/kg, contained greatly elevated whole body Pb burdens of 9 to 18 mg/kg fresh weight (Schmitt et al. 1984). By comparison, the highest Pb concentration recorded to date in the National Biocontaminant Monitoring Program is 6.7 mg/kg fresh weight in whole Mozambique tilapia (Tilapia *mossambica*) from Honolulu in 1979 (Lowe et al. 1985). Catostomids from contaminated portions of the Big River contained elevated blood Pb levels, depressed blood ALAD activity levels, and Pb concentrations in edible tissues exceeding 0.3 mg/kg fresh weight--a level considered hazardous to human health (Schmitt et al. 1984). The Missouri Department of Health later issued an advisory against eating castostomids caught in a 65-km section of the Big River (Czarneski 1985).

Whitefish, *Coregonus* spp., from Pb-contaminated Swedish lakes, showed depressed blood ALAD and blood chemistry derangement when compared to fish from a reference lake--suggesting that Pb affects natural populations of fish in a manner similar to that observed in laboratory studies (Haux et al. 1986).

The significance of organolead residues in aquatic life is unknown, and merits additional research. In Ontario, Canada, about 16% of all fish sampled contained tetraalkyllead compounds, although none were recorded in water, vegetation, or sediments from the collection sites (Chau et al. 1980). Tetramethyllead reportedly was produced from biological and chemical methylation of several inorganic and organic Pb compounds in the aquatic environment, and has been detected at low concentrations in marine mussels, lobsters, and bony fishes (Wong et al. 1981).

AMPHIBIANS AND REPTILES

Tadpoles of bullfrogs (*Rana catesbeiana*) and green frogs (*R. clamitans*) from drainages along highways with different daily average traffic volumes (4,272 to 108,800 vehicles per day) contained elevated amounts of Pb (up to 270 mg/kg dry weight), which were positively correlated with Pb in sediments and with average daily traffic volume. Lead in tadpoles living near highways may contribute to the Pb levels reported in wildlife that eat tadpoles. Diets with amounts of Pb similar to those in tadpoles collected near heavily traveled highways have caused adverse physiological and reproductive effects in some species of birds and mammals (Birdsall et al. 1986). Elevated Pb sconcentrations also were recorded in various species of amphibians and reptiles collected near Pb smelters and mines (Table 5).

BIRDS

In general, Pb concentrations were highest in birds from urban locations (perhaps reflecting greater exposure to automotive and industrial contamination) and in birds near Pb mining and smelting facilities. Lead residues also are greatest in older birds (especially in bone, because of accumulation over time), in sexually mature females, and in waterfowl that have ingested Pb shot pellets (Table 5).

Continued deposition of Pb shot by hunters into wetlands habitats exposes birds to lead. Lead shot is a substantial localized source of contamination, especially in prime waterfowl habitat (Bellrose 1951, 1959; NRCC 1973; White and Stendell 1977; Stendell et al. 1979; Wobeser 1981; Clausen et al. 1982; Longcore et al. 1982; Mudge 1983; Driver and Kendall 1984; Hall and Fisher 1985). Several million hunters are estimated to deposit more than 6,000 metric tons of Pb shot annually into lakes, marshes, and estuaries; this represents about 6,440 pellets per bird bagged. Shot densities as great as 860,000 pellets/ha (2,124,000/acre) have been estimated in some locations (Wobeser 1981), although concentrations of 34,000 to 140,000/ha are more common (Longcore et al. 1982; Driver and Kendall 1984). For example, Pb shot in bottom sediments from Merrymeeting Bay, Maine, a prime waterfowl staging area, averaged 99,932 shot/ha (274,000/acre), and ranged from 59,541 to 140,324/ha; shot were significantly more numerous in silt than in sand sediments. In general, shot sink more rapidly in soft than in firm substrates, and there is only slight carryover of shot from one season to the next in areas with silt or peat bottoms (Wobeser 1981).

Waterfowl and other birds ingest spent shot during feeding and retain them as grit in the gizzard; the pellets are eroded and soluble Pb is absorbed from the digestive tract. In many species, the ingestion of a single pellet is often fatal. Most deaths, however, go unnoticed and unrecorded. Species such as the mallard and pintail that feed in shallow water by sifting through bottom mud are more likely to encounter shot than are species that feed on submerged vegetation or at the surface (Wobeser 1981). Ingested Pb shot was recorded in 6 of 10 duck species; the frequency was 8.1% in American black ducks sampled in Maine during the hunting seasons of 1976 through 1980 (Longcore et al. 1982). In dry seasons, species that probe for food deep in the sediment are especially susceptible (Hall and Fisher 1985). In England, ingested pellets occurred in 3.2% of the total waterfowl in 16 species examined. Incidences of shot were relatively high (7.1% to 11.8%) in four species (Mudge 1983): greylag goose (*Anser anser*), gadwall (*Anas strepera*). pochard (*Aythya ferina*), and tufted duck

(*Aythya fuligula*). At least 8,000 mallards in Britain die each winter of Pb toxicosis from ingestion of spent shot (Mudge 1983). It is estimated that about 2.4 million ducks die worldwide of Pb shot poisoning each year--and this estimate does not include population losses resulting from the sublethal effects of Pb (Wobeser 1981). Among larger species of waterfowl, outbreaks of Pb poisoning have been documented in Canada geese, whistling swans (*Cygnus columbianus*), trumpeter swans, and mute swans (Eskildsen and Grandjean 1984). Lead-poisoned waterfowl tend to seek seclusion and often die in areas of heavy cover; these carcasses are rapidly removed by predators and scavengers, and may result in secondary Pb poisoning, especially among raptors such as the bald eagle (Feierabend and Myers 1984; Reichel et al. 1984). Of 293 bald eagles found dead nationwide between 1978 and 1981, 17 (5.8%) probably died of Pb poisoning after ingesting hunter-killed or hunter-crippled waterfowl containing Pb pellets (Reichel et al. 1984).

The relation between embedded shot and lead toxicosis is unclear. The incidence of embedded shot in various species of waterfowl ranged from 11% to 43% in adults, and 2% to 11% in immatures (Perry and Artmann 1979; Perry and Geissler 1980). Many birds that were struck by shotgun pellets but survived may have died prematurely or been eaten by predators. In one study, the bodies of 23% of adult Atlantic brant (*Branta bernicla hrota*) that died from starvation in New Jersey in 1977 contained embedded lead shot (Kirby et al. 1983). The effects on survival and fecundity of receiving and carrying relatively high frequencies of embedded shot might be significant, and during years of low adult numbers might have substantial population consequences (Kirby et al. 1983).

Lead in seeds and invertebrates within rights-of-way of major highways probably is not a hazard to adult ground-foraging songbirds, as judged from experiments with the European starling (*Sturnus vulgaris*). However, the effects of Pb on survival of fledglings are unknown, although Pb causes reductions in blood hemoglobin, hematocrit, ALAD activity, and brain weight (Grue et al. 1986). In another study, Pb concentrations in feather, carcass, and stomach contents of adult and nestling barn swallows (*Hirundo rustica*) were greater near a major U.S. highway than in a rural area; however, the number of eggs and nestlings, the body weight of nestlings at 17 days of age, and body weights of adults were similar in the two colonies, suggesting that contamination of roadsides with Pb from automobile emissions is not a major hazard to birds that feed on flying invertebrates (Grue et al. 1984).

Signs of Pb poisoning, i.e., depressed blood ALAD activity or elevated blood Pb levels, were reported for birds near a metal smelter (Beyer et al. 1985), in 17% of canvasbacks from Chesapeake Bay in 1974 (Dieter et al. 1976), and in three species of waders from the Dutch Wadden Sea living in an urban postnuptial moulting area (Goede and de Voogt 1985). The decline in submerged aquatic vegetation in Chesapeake Bay and the later shift in diet of some waterfowl species of Chesapeake Bay from the vegetation (Pb content 2.2 to 18.9 mg/kg dry weight), to the softshell clam *Mya arenaria* (1.3 to 7.6 mg Pb/kg dry weight), or to other bivalve molluscs (0.8 to 20.4 mg Pb/kg dry weight), probably did not increase dietary Pb burdens in these species (Di Guilio and Scanlon 1985).

The significance of trace amounts of organolead residues in birds is unknown. Trialkyllead seems to concentrate in avian kidney, but contributes less than 5% of the total amount of Pb in kidneys (Johnson et al. 1982).

MAMMALS

The highest body burdens of Pb reported in mammals were near urban areas of dense vehicular traffic, near metal mines and smelters, or near plants that reclaimed storage batteries; concentrations were higher in older organisms, especially in bone and hematopoietic tissues (Table 5; Goldsmith and Scanlon 1977; Way and Schroder 1982). A similar pattern of Pb occurrence and distribution was evident for human populations (Barth et al. 1973).

Diet provides the major pathway for Pb exposure, and amounts in bone are indicative of estimated Pb exposure and metabolism (Chmiel and Harrison 1981). Amounts of whole body Pb and feeding habits of roadside rodents were correlated: body burdens were highest in insectivores such as shrews; intermediate in herbivores, and lowest in granivores (Boggess 1977; Getz et al. 1977c). Food chain biomagnification of Pb, although uncommon in terrestrial communities, may be important for carnivorous marine mammals, such as the California sea lion (*Zalophus californianus*); accumulations were 52 highest in hard tissues, such as bone and teeth, and lowest in soft tissues, such as fat and muscle (Braham 1973). A similar pattern was observed in the

41

harbor seal, *Phoca vitulina* (Roberts et al. 1976).

The most sensitive index of Pb intoxication in populations of deer mice was the formation of acid-fast-staining intranuclear inclusion bodies within proximal convoluted tubule cells of kidney; secondary indicators included decreased body weight, renal edema, reticulocytosis, increased urinary ALA excretion, and decreased hematocrit (Mierau and Favara 1975). Mierau and Favara (1975) concluded that Pb pollution from automobile exhausts has had little impact on deer mice, and that severe Pb poisoning is unlikely at traffic densities below 200,000 vehicles per day. Others, however, believe that Pb emissions from automotive exhausts may pose unnecessary risks to various species of bats, rodents, and mule deer (*Odocoileus hemionus*). Estimated doses of Pb ingested by the little brown bat (*Myotis lucifugus*) and highway populations of shrews and voles equaled or exceeded dosages that have caused death or reproductive impairment in domestic animals; further, mean Pb concentrations in bats and shrews near highways exceed those reported for small rodents with Pb-induced renal abnormalities collected from abandoned Pb-mining sites (Clark 1979). Mule deer from the Rocky Mountain National Park, Colorado, that graze on (heavily contaminated) roadside forage must consume 1.4% of their daily intake from roadsides before harmful amounts of Pb (3 mg Pb/day) are obtained (Harrison and Dyer 1984); however, this value needs to be verified.

Cows (*Bos bovis*) adjacent to a Pb battery reclamation plant showed signs of Pb toxicosis, including muscle tremors, blindness, dribbling urine, and drooling. Mice trapped within 400 m of the plant had acid-fast-staining intranuclear inclusions in renal tubular epithelial cells--a useful diagnostic indicator of Pb poisoning. A faulty air pollution control system at the plant caused deposition of particulate Pb on the cornfield used for cattle forage, and was the probable source of the Pb toxicosis in the animals (Kisseberth et al. 1984). Industrial airborne Pb pollution is responsible for contamination of cattle and horses (*Equus caballus*) within 1,000 m of the source, resulting in elevated blood Pb levels in both species, stillbirths and abortions in cattle, and some deaths in horses (Edwards and Clay 1977).

Proximity to the smokestacks of metal smelters is positively associated with increased levels of Pb in the hair (manes) of horses and in tissues of small mammals, and is consistent with the results of soil and vegetation analyses (EPA 1972). Lead concentrations were comparatively high in the hair of older or chronically impaired horses (EPA 1972). However, tissues of white-tailed deer (*Odocoileus virginianus*) collected near a zinc smelter did not contain elevated levels of Pb (Sileo and Beyer 1985). Among small mammals near a metal smelter, blood ALAD activity was reduced in the white-footed mouse but normal in others, e.g., the short-tailed shrew (Beyer et al. 1985). The interaction effects of Pb components in smelter emissions with other components, such as zinc, cadmium, and arsenic, are unresolved (EPA 1972), and warrant additional research.

LETHAL AND SUBLETHAL EFFECTS

GENERAL

Lead adversely affects survival, growth, reproduction, development, and metabolism of most species under controlled conditions, but its effects are substantially modified by numerous physical, chemical, and biological variables. In general, organolead compounds are more toxic than inorganic Pb compounds, food chain biomagnification of Pb is negligible, and the younger, immature organisms are most susceptible. Uptake of Pb by terrestrial plants is limited by the low bioavailability of Pb from soils; adverse effects seem to occur only at total concentrations of several hundred mg Pb/kg soil.

In aquatic environments, waterborne Pb was the most toxic form. Adverse effects were noted on daphnid reproduction at 1.0 ug Pb^{2+}/1, on rainbow trout survival at 3.5 ug tetraethyllead/l, and on growth of marine algae at 5.1 ug Pb^{2+}/1. High bioconcentration factors were recorded for filter-feeding bivalve molluscs and freshwater algae at 5.0 ug Pb^{2+}/1.

Ingestion of spent lead shot by migratory waterfowl and other birds is a significant cause of mortality in these species, and also in raptors that eat the waterfowl killed or wounded by hunters. Forms of Pb other than shot are unlikely to cause clinical signs of Pb poisoning in birds, except for certain alkyllead compounds that bioconcentrate in aquatic food items. Among sensitive species of birds, survival was reduced at doses of 75 to 150 mg Pb^{2+}/kg BW or 28 mg alkyllead/kg BW, reproduction was impaired at dietary levels of 50 mg Pb^{2+}/kg, and signs of poisoning were evident at doses as low as 2.8 mg alkyllead/kg BW.

The veterinary medical literature on Pb toxicosis is abundant for domestic livestock and small laboratory animals, but notably lacking for feral mammals. Among sensitive species of mammals, survival was reduced at acute oral doses as low as 5 mg/kg BW in the rat, at chronic oral doses of 0.3 mg/kg BW in the dog, and at dietary levels of 1.7 mg Pb/kg BW in the horse. Sublethal effects were documented in monkeys given doses as low as 0.1 mg Pb/kg BW daily (impaired learning 2 years postadministration), or fed diets containing 0.5 mg Pb/kg (abnormal social behavior). Reduction in ALAD activity was recorded in blood of rabbits given 0.005 mg Pb/kg BW, and in mice given 0.05 mg Pb/kg BW. Tissue residues increased in mice given 0.03 mg Pb/kg BW, and in sheep given 0.05 mg Pb/kg BW.

TERRESTRIAL PLANTS AND INVERTEBRATES

Fruits and vegetables acquire Pb by surface deposition from rainfall, dust, and soil, and by biological uptake through the root system (EPA 1980). Foliar absorption of Pb and transport to the root could account for a significant portion of the Pb in root tissues; however, this transport process varies widely among species. Dollard (1986) showed that this pathway accounted for 35% of the root Pb content in the radish (*Raphanus sativus*), but for <3% in carrots (*Daucus carota*) and beans (*Phaseolus vulgaris*). Corn (*Zea mays*) contained 30 mg Pb/kg dry weight when grown in soils containing Pb concentrations of 924 mg/kg, but only 17 mg/kg when grown in soils containing 786 mg Pb/kg. Sadiq (1985) concluded that contamination of soils with up to 800 mg Pb/kg probably does not elevate concentrations of Pb in corn plants. Within any plant species, however, there are Pb-resistant and Pb-sensitive breeds; some genetically fixed resistant species grow in soils containing up to 10,000 mg Pb/kg (Holl and Hampp 1975).

Plants readily accumulate Pb from soils of low pH or low organic content; however, uptake is significantly reduced after the application of lime or phosphate, which converts Pb to hydroxides, carbonates, or phosphates of relatively low solubility (Demayo et al. 1982). Lead persists for lengthy periods in forest litter; the estimated Tb 1/2 is 220 years (Turner et al. 1985). Lead seems to be tightly bound by most soils, and substantial amounts must accumulate before it affects the growth of higher plants (Boggess 1977). Although Pb is preferentially bound in soils by organics and oxides, interaction kinetics of Pb with other metals are complex and largely unknown (Bjerre and Schierup 1985). For example, uptake of Pb from soils by oat seeds (*Avena sativa*) was inhibited by cadmium salts, and reduced in loamy or organic soils; further, Pb in soils interfered with manganese uptake, and also increased the availability of cadmium and other heavy metals (Bjerre and Schierup 1985).

Lead inhibits plant growth, reduces photosynthesis, and reduces mitosis and water absorption (Demayo et al. 1982). Inhibition of photosynthesis is attributed to the blocking of protein sulfhydryl groups and to changes in phosphate levels in living cells (Holl and Hampp 1975). For two species of roadside weeds (*Cassia* spp.), pollen germination was reduced by 90% and seed germination by 87% at Pb levels of about 500 mg/kg dry weight in soil and about 300 mg/kg dry weight in foliage (Krishnayya and Bedi 1986). Normal germination rates were recorded at Pb levels of 46 mg/kg in soil and 22 mg/kg dry weight in foliage; however, some adverse effects were evident at Pb levels of 12 to 312 mg/kg in soil, and 55 to 97 mg/kg dry weight in foliage (Krishnayya and Bedi 1986). Tetraethyllead from automobile exhaust fumes is known to react in the light to produce the highly phytotoxic triethyllead cation (Backhaus and Backhaus 1986), which can freely permeate the plasma membranes of plant cells (Stournaras et al. 1984). Growth of cultures of soybean (*Glycine max*) cells exposed to 207 ug Pb/1 (as triethyllead salts) was inhibited before the cells died (Stournaras et al. 1984). There is no 56 evidence for biomagnification of Pb in the food chain of vegetation, to cattle, to dung, to the dung beetle (Robel et al. 1981), nor is there convincing evidence that any terrestrial vegetation is important in food chain biomagnification of Pb (EPA 1980).

Concentrations of Pb in soil litter ranged from 3,200 mg/kg in locations near a zinc smelter in Palmerton, Pennsylvania, to 150 mg/kg at sites 105 km distant; relative concentrations of cadmium, zinc, and copper were similar (Beyer et al. 1984). In woodlice (*Porcellio scaber*) fed litter from these locales for 8 weeks, survival decreased as metal content in the litter increased, but the major cause of death was zinc poisoning and not Pb poisoning (Beyer et al. 1984). Woodlouse (*Oniscus asellus*) hepatopancreas that were collected 3 km downwind of a metal smelter contained large amounts of zinc, copper, cadmium and Pb. Centipedes (*Lithobius variegatus*) that ate woodlice hepatopancreas did not assimilate Pb even though the food contained concentrations that were many times greater than normally encountered (Hopkin and Martin 1984). However, survival and reproduction were reduced in woodlice (*P. scaber*) fed soil litter treated with 12,800 mg Pb/kg, as lead oxide, for 64 weeks, or two generations (Beyer and Anderson 1985). This amount of Pb is similar to the amounts reportedly associated with reductions in natural populations of decomposers, such as fungi, earthworms, and arthropods. The poisoning of decomposers may disrupt nutrient cycling, reduce the number of invertebrates available to other wildlife for food, and contribute to food chain contamination (Beyer and Anderson 1985). The effects of Pb on soil microbial populations is unknown (Boggess 1977).

Herbivorous land snails (*Helix* spp.) are important in Pb cycling through contaminated ecosystems (Dallinger and Wieser 1984; Beeby 1985). *Helix pomatia* fed lettuce enriched with Pb (about 1,000 mg Pb/kg dry weight lettuce) for 32 days contained 1,301 mg Pb/kg dry weight in the mid-gut gland (vs. 52 in controls), and much lower amounts (<30 mg/kg) in other tissues. After the snail had fed on uncontaminated lettuce for 50 days, Pb remained elevated at 1,203 mg,/kg in the mid-gut gland, which contained more than 90% of the total body burden (Dallinger and Wieser 1984).

AQUATIC BIOTA

In general, the responses of aquatic species to Pb insult differed markedly (Table 6). Among sensitive species, however, several trends were evident: (1) dissolved waterborne Pb was more toxic than total Pb; (2) organic lead compounds were more toxic than inorganic forms; (3) adverse effects on daphnid reproduction were evident at 1.0 ug Pb^{2+} /l; (4) high bioconcentrations were measured in oysters at 1.0 ug Pb /1 and in freshwater algae at 5.0 ug Pb^{2+} /l; (5) tetramethyllead was acutely toxic to rainbow trout at 3.5 ug/l; (6) growth inhibition of a marine alga was reported at 5.1 ug Pb^{2+} /1; and (7) for all species, effects were most pronounced at elevated water temperatures and reduced pH, in comparatively soft waters, in younger life stages, and after long exposures (Table 6).

Table 6. Lethal and sublethal effects of lead[a] to selected species of aquatic organisms.

Ecosystem, taxonomic group, species, and other variables	Concentration (µg Pb/L medium)	Exposure duration	Effect[b]	Reference[c]
Freshwater				
Algae and macrophytes				
Alga, *Selenastrum capricornutum*	5	28 days	BCF 92,000	1
Alga, *S. capricornutum*	50	28 days	BCF 26,000	1
Alga, *Chlamydomonas reinhardii*	207	3 h	BCF 26; some inhibition of photosynthesis	2
Alga, *C. reinhardii*	1,000	3 h	BCF 20; 50% inhibition of photosynthesis	2
Alga, *C. reinhardii*	4,140	24 h	Lethal	2
Alga, *Microcystis aeruginosa*	450	8 days	Immobilization	3
Invertebrates				
Daphnid, *Daphnia magna*	1	19 days	Reproductive impairment, 10%	4
Daphnid, *D. magna*	10	19 days	Reproductive impairment, 50%	4
Daphnid, *D. magna*	30	21 days	Reproductive impairment, 16%	3, 5
Water hardness (mg $CaCO_3$/L)				
52	9–16.7	Lifetime	MATC	3
102	78–181	Lifetime	MATC	3
151	85–193	Lifetime	MATC	3
54	612	96 h	LC-50	3

110	952	96 h	LC-50	3
152	1,910	96 h	LC-50	3
45	300	21 days	LC-50	6, 7
45	450	48 h	Immobilization, 50%	3, 7
Snail, *Lymnaea palustris*	12–54	Lifetime	MATC	3
Snail, *L. palustris*	3.8	Lifetime	No deaths	8
Snail, *L. palustris*	19	Lifetime	Significant mortality	8
Snail, *L. palustris*	36	Lifetime	Reduction in biomass, 50%	8
Snail, *L. palustris*	48	Lifetime	Reduction in biomass, 100%	8
Snail, *L. palustris*	54	Lifetime	Hatching success reduced; survivors dead by age 80 days	8
Protozoan, *Entosiphon sulcatum*	20	72 h	Immobilization	3
Amphipod, *Gammarus pseudolimnaeus*	28.4	60 days	LC-50	5
Amphipod *G. pseudolimnaeus*	124	96 h	LC-50	9
Aquatic invertebrates	32	28 days	BCF 1,000 to 9,000	5
Protozoan, *Uronema* sp.	70	20 h	Immobilization	3
Midge, *Tanytarsus dissimilis*	258	10 days	LC-50	3
Isopod, *Asellus meridianus*				
Nontolerant strain	280	48 h	LC-50	5
From Pb-contaminated river	3,500	48 h	LC-50	5
Daphnid, *Daphnia hyalina*	600	48 h	LC-50	6
Snail, *Viviparus ater*	1,000	7 days	Neuronal cytolysis	10
Snail, *V. ater*	117,000	96 h	LC-50	10
Aquatic insects, 5 species	3,500 to 64,000	7 to 14 days	LC-50	5
Isopod, *Asellus aquaticus*				
Nontolerant strain				
Pretreated for 5 days to 100 mg Pb/L	794,000	48 h	LC-50	11
No pretreatment	330,000	48 h	LC-50	11
Fish				
Rainbow trout, *Salmo gairdneri*				
Tetramethyl Pb				
Weight 1 gram	3.5	72 h	LC-50	12
Weight 1 gram	3.5	7 days	BCF 726 for whole trout	12
Weight 1 gram	3.5	14 days	LC-50	12
Weight 20 grams	24	8 to 14 days	Some deaths at day 8; BCF 17,300 for intestinal lipids at day 10 and 12,540 at day 14	

Pb^{2+}	13	32 weeks	Anemia; reduced blood ALAD activity	3
Pb^{2+}	14	14 days	Reduced stamina	3
Pb^{2+}	10	30 days	ALAD depression, 21%	13
Pb^{2+}	75	30 days	ALAD depression, 74%	13
Pb^{2+}	300	30 days + 7 weeks post-exposure	ALAD depression, 86%; anemia; basophilic stippling of erythrocytes	13
Pb^{2+}	13	4 weeks	Erythrocyte ALAD inhibition	6
Eyed eggs	10,000	56 h	LC-50	14
Eyed eggs	20,000	20 h	LC-50	14
Water hardness (mg $CaCO_3$/L)				
28				
Total Pb	7.2–14.6	Lifetime	MATC	15
Dissolved	4.1–7.6	Lifetime	MATC	15
Dissolved Pb	1,200	96 h	LC-50	5
35	71–146	Lifetime	MATC	3
353				
Total Pb	506,500	96 h	LC-50	15
Dissolved Pb	1395	96 h	LC-50	15
Dissolved Pb	120–360	Lifetime	MATC	15
Dissolved Pb	18.2–31.7	Lifetime	MATC	15
28				
Pre-hatch fry	4–7.6	Lifetime	MATC	5
Post-hatch fry	7.6–14.6	Lifetime	MATC	5
28	14.6	19 months	Vertebral deformities; caudal fin erosion	6
353	31	19 months	As above	6
28	7.2	19 months	No harmful effects	6
353	18.2	19 months	As above	6
Lake trout, *Salvelinus namaycush*				
Water hardness 33	48–83	Lifetime	MATC	16
Zebrafish, *Brachydanio rerio*				
Egg	50	24 h	Pigmentation patterns of fry irreversibly altered	17
Egg	72	24 h	Hatching inhibited	17
Brook trout, *Salvelinus fontinalis*				
Water hardness 44				
Total Pb	58–119	3 generations	MATC	3, 5, 18
Dissolved Pb	39–84	3 generations	MATC	5, 18
Total Pb	4,100	96 h	LC-50	18

Dissolved Pb	3,362	96 h	LC-50	18
Total Pb	134	21 days	Growth reduction	6
Total Pb	119	3 generations	First generation: BCF 571 for liver and 1,806 for kidney. Second generation: BCF 420 for liver, 1,504 for kidney; severe spinal deformities in 34%. Third generation: spinal deformities in 21%, reduction in body weight	18
Total Pb	235	2 generations	All with spinal deformities	18
Bluegill, *Lepomis macrochirus*				
Water hardness 41	70–120	Lifetime	MATC	16
Channel catfish, *Ictalurus punctatus*				
Water hardness 36	75–136	Lifetime	MATC	16
White sucker, *Catostomus commersoni*				
Water hardness 34	119–253	Lifetime	MATC	5
Cyprinid, *Puntius conchonius*	127	4 months	Gonadal pathology	19
Cyprinid, *P. conchonius*	379	96 h	LC-50	19
Goldfish, *Carassius auratus*	200	4–5 days	ALAD inhibition	6
Northern pike, *Esox lucius*				
Water hardness 34 (mg $CaCO_3$/L)	253–483	Lifetime	MATC	5
Threespine stickleback, *Gasterosteus aculeatus*	300	96 h	LC-100	6
Smallmouth bass, *Micropterus dolomieui*				
Water hardness 152 (mg $CaCO_3$/L)				
Fingerlings	405	90 days	No effect on growth, behavior, blood chemistry	20
Swim-up fry	2,800	96 h	LC-50	20
Fingerlings	29,000	96 h	LC-50	20
Egg and sac-fry	>15,900	96 h	LC-50	20
Fathead minnow, *Pimephales promelas*				
Water hardness (mg $CaCO_3$/L)				
20	6,500	96 h	LC-50	7
360	460,000	96 h	LC-50	7

Marine

Algae and macrophytes

Diatom, *Skeletonema costatum*	0.05	12 days	No effect on growth	21
Diatom, *S. costatum*	5.1	12 days	Growth inhibition, 50%	3
Diatom, *S. costatum*	10	12 days	Growth inhibition, 100%	21
Alga, *Phaeodactylum tricornutum*				
Pb^{2+}	20	<1 h	BCF 582,000	22
Pb^{2+}	>5,000	96 h	LC-50	23
Tetramethyl Pb1	1,300	96 h	LC-50	23
Trimethyl Pb	800	96 h	LC-50	23
Triethyl Pb	100	96 h	LC-50	23
Tetraethyl Pb	100	96 h	LC-50	23
Phytoplankton, mixed populations	21	4 days	Reduced biomass	3
Alga, *Dunaliella tertiolecta*				
Tetraethyl Pb	150	96 h	Growth inhibition	3
Tetramethyl Pb	1,650	96 h	Growth inhibition	3

Invertebrates

American oyster, *Crassostrea virginica*, soft parts	1.0	140 days	BCF 6,600	24
American oyster, soft parts	3.3	140 days	BCF 3,454	24
Blue mussel, *Mytilus edulis*				
Pb^{2+}, adults	>500,000	96 h	LC-50	23
Pb^{2+}, larvae	476	96 h	LC-50	3
Triethyl Pb	1,100	96 h	LC-50; BCF 10	23
Trimethyl Pb	500	96 h	LC-50; BCF 23	23
Tetramethyl Pb	270	96 h	LC-50; BCF 170	23
Tetraethyl Pb	100	96 h	LC-50; BCF 120	23
Pb^{2+}	10	63 days	BCF 12,580 for kidney and 1,580 for soft parts	25
Pb^{2+}	500	150 days	BCF 25,670 for soft parts	26

Softshell clam, *Mya arenaria*

Soft parts

Temperature, °C

0–10	14	42 days	BCF 158	27
0–10	70	42 days	BCF 180	27
16–22	14	14 days	BCF 351	27
16–22	70	7 days	BCF 237	27
Mysid, *Mysidopsis bahia*	17–37	Lifetime	MATC	3

Sandworm, *Neanthes arenaceodentata*

Salinity, o/oo				
15	20	23 days	Inhibited reproduction	28
20	3,100	28 days	Inhibited reproduction	28
Temperature, °C				
15	10,700	96 h	LC-50	28
20	7,700	96 h	LC-50	28
Shrimp, *Crangon crangon*				
Pb^{2+}	375,000	96 h	LC-50	23
Trimethyl Pb	8,800	96 h	LC-50; BCF 1	23
Triethyl Pb	5,800	96 h	LC-50; BCF 2	23
Tetramethyl Pb	110	96 h	LC-50; BCF 20	23
Tetraethyl Pb	20	96 h	LC-50; BCF 650	23
American lobster,				
Homarus americanus	50	30 days	Reduced ALAD activity	3
American lobster	50	30 days	Biochemical alterations in antennal gland; BCF 2,760 for antennal gland, and 58 for gill	29
Protozoan, *Cristigera* sp.	150	12 h	Reduced growth	3
Amphipod, *Ampelisca abdita*	547	96 h	LC-50	3
Dungeness crab,				
Cancer magister	575	96 h	LC-50	38
Sea urchin, *Anthocidaris*				
crassispina (embryos)	1,100	48 h	No effect on development	30
Sea urchin (embryos)	2,200	48 h	Development inhibited	30
Fish				
Plaice, *Pleuronectes platessa*				
Tetramethyl Pb	50	96 h	LC-50; BCF 60	23
Tetraethyl Pb	230	96 h	LC-50; BCF 130	23
Triethyl Pb	1,700	96 h	LC-50; BCF 2	23
Trimethyl Pb	24,600	96 h	LC-50; BCF 1	23
Diethyl Pb	75,000	96 h	LC-50	23
Pb^{2+}	180,000	96 h	LC-50	23
Dimethyl Pb	300,000	96 h	LC-50	23
Mummichog, *Fundulus heteroclitus*	315	96 h	LC-50	3

[a]As total Pb, unless indicated otherwise.

[b]BCF = bioconcentration factor; MATC = maximum acceptable toxicant concentration. Lower value in each MATC pair indicates highest concentration tested producing no measurable effect on growth, survival, reproduction, and metabolic upset during chronic exposure; higher value indicates lowest concentration tested producing a measurable effect.

CReferences: 1, Vighi 1981; 2, Irmer et al. 1986; 3, EPA 1985; 4, Berglind et al. 1985; 5, Demayo et al. 1982; 6, Wong et al. 1978; 7, NRCC 1973; 8, Borgmann et al. 1978; 9, Spehar et al. 1978; 10, Fantin et al. 1985; 11, Fraser 1980; 12, Wong et al. 1981; 13, Johansson-Sjobeck and Larsson 1979; 14, Rombaugh 1985; 15, Davies et al. 1976; 16, EPA 1980; 17, Ozoh 1980; 18, Holcombe et al. 1976; 19, Kumar and Pant 1984; 20, Coughlan et al. 1986; 21, Rivkin 1979; 22, Schulz-Baldes and Lewin 1976; 23, Maddock and Taylor 1980; 24, Zaroogian et al. 1979; 25, Schulz-Baldes 1974; 26, Schulz-Baldes 1972; 27, Eisler 1977; 28, Reish and Gerlinger 1984; 29, Gould and Grieg 1983; 30, Kobayashi 1971.

Lead is toxic to all phyla of aquatic biota, but its toxic action is modified by species and physiological state, and by physical and chemical variables. Wong et al. (1978) stated that only soluble waterborne Pb is toxic to aquatic biota, and that free cationic forms are more toxic than complexed forms. The biocidal properties of soluble Pb are also modified significantly by water hardness: as hardness increased, Pb becomes less bioavailable because of precipitation increases (NRCC 1973). In salmonids, for example, the toxicity and fate of Pb are influenced by the calcium status of the organism, and this relation may account for the reduced effects of Pb in hard or estuarine waters. In coho salmon (*Oncorhynchus kisutch*), an increase in waterborne or dietary calcium reduced uptake and retention of Pb in skin and skeleton (Varanasi and Gmur 1978).

Organolead compounds are, in general, more toxic than inorganic Pb compounds to aquatic organisms. Ethyl derivatives were more toxic than methyl derivatives, and toxicity increased with increasing degree of alkylation, tetralkyllead being the most toxic (Chau et al. 1980). Tetraethyllead was about 10X more effective than tetramethyllead in reducing oxygen consumption by coastal marine bacteria, and was 1.5 to 4X more toxic than tetramethyllead to marine teleosts (Marchetti 1978). Tetramethyllead chloride was 20X as toxic as $Pb(NO_3)_2$ to freshwater algae, and 2X as toxic as trimethyllead acetate (Wong et al. 1978). In seawater, the release of tetraalkyllead compounds is more likely than accumulation to result in acutely toxic effects; however, alkyllead compounds degrade rapidly to trialkyllead chlorides, which are only 0.1 to 0.01 as toxic as TEL compounds (Haddock and Taylor 1980). Alkyllead compounds are accumulated more readily by freshwater teleosts than are inorganic Pb compounds. The BCF values for tetramethyllead and rainbow trout, for example, ranged from 124 in lipids after exposure for 1 day, to 934 after 7 days (Demayo et al. 1982). Depuration of tetramethyllead is rapid; the estimated Tb 1/2 values range from 30 hours for intestinal lipids to 45 hours for skin and cephalic fat deposits (Wong et al. 1981). Some microorganisms in lake sediments transform certain inorganic and organic Pb compounds into the more toxic tetramethyllead, but the pathways are not well understood (Wong et al. 1978).

Lethal solutions of Pb (as well as of many other heavy metals) cause increased mucous formation in fishes. The excess coagulates over the entire body and is particularly prominent over the gills, interfering with respiratory function and resulting in death by anoxia (Aronson 1971; NRCC 1973). Increasing waterborne concentrations of Pb over 10 ug/l are expected to provide increasingly severe long-term effects on fish and fisheries (Demayo et al. 1982). Fish that are continuously exposed to toxic concentrations of waterborne Pb show various signs of Pb poisoning: spinal curvature, usually as lordosis; anemia; darkening of the dorsal tail region, producing a black-tail effect due to selective destruction of chromatophores but not of melanophores; degeneration of the caudal fin; destruction of spinal neurons; ALAD inhibition in erythrocytes, spleen, liver, and renal tissues; reduced ability to swim against a current; destruction of the respiratory epithelium; basophilic stippling of erythrocytes; elevated Pb concentrations in blood, bone, gill, liver, and kidney; muscular atrophy; paralysis; renal pathology; growth inhibition; retardation of sexual maturity; altered blood chemistry; testicular and ovarian histopathology; and death (Aronson 1971; NRCC 1973; Adams 1975; Davies et al. 1976; Holcombe et al. 1976; Hodson et al. 1977, 1980, 1982; Johansson-Sjobeck and Larsson 1979; Reichert et al. 1979; Ozoh 1980; Demayo et al 1982; Kumar and Pant 1984; Rai and Qayyum 1984; Hodson and Spry 1985; Haux et al. 1986). The prevalence of signs is closely correlated with duration of exposure to Pb and to its uptake (Hodson et al 1982). Toxic effects of Pb uptake in fishes are increased under conditions favoring their rapid growth. Hodson et al. (1982) have shown that the rate of intoxication by Pb--as judged by uptake rates into tissues and incidence and prevalence of black tail--did not increase with fish size, but rather with growth rate.

Rooted aquatic plants, such as wild rice (*Zizania aquatica*), can accumulate up to 67 mg Pb/kg dry weight when cultured in tanks contaminated with high concentrations of powdered Pb (equivalent to 7,400 kg Pb/ha);

however, this level is not considered hazardous to waterfowl feeding on wild rice (Behan et al. 1979). Lead content in plants collected from heavily hunted areas near refuges did not differ from those collected in the protected areas (Behan et al. 1979), which suggests that Pb bioavailability to rooted aquatics is substantially lower from shot than from powdered Pb. In another study with rooted macrophytes, *Navicula* sp. and *Elodea canadensis* rapidly accumulated Pb from solutions containing 1.0 mg Pb^{2+} /l, i.e., 70 mg Pb/kg dry weight per minute; the process was overwhelmingly passive (Everard and Denny 1985). Depuration was rapid; 90% of the Pb sorbed during the first hour by shoots of *Elodea* was released within 14 days after transfer to clean water, though 10% seemed to be irreversibly bound (Everard and Denny 1985).

High accumulations of Pb from ambient seawater by marine plants is well documented; concentration factors vary from 13,000 to 82,000 for algae from Raritan Bay, New Jersey (Seeliger and Edwards 1977), and from 1,200 to 26,000 for algae from Sorfjorden, Norway (Melhuus et al. 1978). Studies on the kinetics of lead uptake and retention in two species of marine algae (*Phaeodactylum tricornutum, Platymonas subcordiformes*) showed that both species accumulated Pb from the medium at ambient concentrations of 20 ug/l, and higher (Schulz-Baldes and Lewin 1976). In the first phase, usually completed within minutes after addition of Pb, cells of *Phaeodactylum* became saturated when the Pb reached a remarkable 11,640 mg/kg dry weight. In the second phase, the lead content of *Platymonas* continued to rise slowly, but that of *Phaeodactylum* declined after 2 or 3 days. In both species the content of bound Pb increased with increasing exposure time, suggesting that during prolonged exposure Pb is initially adsorbed to the cell surface, then translocated into the cell wall, the plasma membrane, and eventually the cytoplasm (Schulz-Baldes and Lewin 1976).

Sediments are not only sinks for Pb but may act as a source of Pb to aquatic biota after contamination from the original source has subsided (Knowlton et al. 1983). The uptake of Pb from artificially contaminated pond sediments was recorded in roots and foliage of submersed aquatic macrophytes (*Potamogeton foliosus, Najus guadalupensis*) and in the exoskeleton of crayfish (*Orconectes nais*). Accumulation of Pb in crayfish primarily was through adsorption; most was lost through molting, though some internal uptake and elimination occurred without molting (Knowlton et al. 1983). Crustacean molts represent 15% of the Pb body burden and are probably more significant than fecal pellets in Pb cycling processes (Fowler 1977).

Median BCF values in aquatic biota exposed to various concentrations of Pb^{2+} for 14 to 140 days varied from about 42 in fish to 2,570 in mussels; intermediate values were 536 for oysters, 500 for insects, 725 for algae, and 1,700 for snails (EPA 1985). There are several notable exceptions to this array: significantly higher values have been reported in crustacean hepatopancreas (Heyraud and Cherry 1979), in various species of freshwater invertebrates (Spehar et al. 1978), in fish bone (Demayo et al. 1982) and liver (Haux and Larsson 1982), and in whole oysters (Zaroogian et al. 1979). In oysters, for example, BCF values varied from 3,450 to 6,600 after exposure to solutions containing 1.0 to 3.3 ug Pb^{2+} /1 for 140 days, but oysters and their progeny were apparently unaffected at whole body burdens (less shell) up to 11.4 mg Pb/kg dry weight (Zaroogian et al. 1979). Many species of aquatic biota contain Pb in amounts >1,000 mg/kg fresh weight (>10,000 mg/kg dry weight) including some marine seaweeds, freshwater macrophytes and algae, annelids, crustaceans, echinoderms, molluscs, and teleosts (Wong et al. 1978); presumably, the Pb was sorbed passively and little, if any, was incorporated biologically. Variations in Pb concentrations in aquatic biota probably reflect the ability of individual species to adsorb waterborne Pb, and may be a direct function of the ratio of surface to body weight (Demayo et al. 1982). The residence time of Pb in aquatic biota seems to be related to the route of administration: Tb 1/2 values were 9 days by waterborne routes and 40 days by diet (Vighi 1981).

Although Pb is concentrated by biota from water, there is no convincing evidence that it is transferred through food chains (Branica and Konrad 1980; Settle and Patterson 1980). Lead concentrations tended to decrease markedly with increasing trophic level in both detritus-based and grazing aquatic food chains (Wong et al. 1978). In the marine food chain of seawater (<0.08 ug Pb/1), to a brown alga (*Egregia laevigata*), to the red abalone (*Haliotis rufescens*), Pb concentrations in the alga and abalone were both <0.04 mg Pb/kg fresh weight after 6 months, indicating negligible biomagnification (Stewart and Schulz-Baldes 1976). When seawater contained 1,000 ug Pb/l, young abalones that fed on *Egregia* for 6 months contained up to 21 mg Pb/kg fresh weight, but neither growth nor activity was affected; Pb selectively accumulated in the digestive gland (38 mg/kg), and was lowest in muscle (<l mg/kg)--the part normally consumed by humans (Stewart and Schulz-Baldes 1976). In the freshwater food chain of an alga (*Selenastrum capricornutum*), to a daphnid (*Daphnia magna*), to the guppy (*Poecilia reticulata*), Pb accumulation progressively decreased from the alga to the guppy.

Thus, in organisms held for 28 days in solutions containing 5 ug Pb/l, Pb content was 460 mg/kg dry weight in the alga, 23 mg/kg in the grazing daphnids, and 4 to 16 mg/kg in the guppies that fed on the daphnids (Vighi 1981). Concentrations of Pb in the freshwater snail, *Lymnaea peregra*, collected near an abandoned Pb mine were positively correlated with the Pb content in its diet; the digestive glands contained up to 5,600 mg/kg dry weight (Everard and Denny 1984). The gut contents of eels (*Anguilla anguilla*) grazing on contaminated snails contained up to 4,350 mg Pb/kg, but the Pb was rapidly released; feces from both snails and eels return the Pb to the ecosystem as particulates and detritus (Everard and Denny 1984).

As discussed earlier, Pb clearly inhibits the formation of heme at several points, adversely affects blood chemistry, and accumulates in hematopoietic organs of aquatic organisms. In addition, Pb interferes with chlorophyll formation in plants by inhibiting the conversion of coproporphyrinogen to proporphyrinogen by competing with iron, inhibits allantoise formation in annelids, inhibits alpha-glycerophosphate dehydrogenase activity in trout, increases glutamic oxalacetate transaminase activity in *Daphnia*, affects neural and hormonal systems that control activity and metabolic rates in fish, interacts with polar sites of glycoproteins in epidermal mucous of fish, and may inhibit vitamin C and tryptophan metabolism (Wong et al. 1978).

Some populations of freshwater isopods are tolerant to Pb. Inasmuch as nontolerant isopods from an unpolluted site can be made tolerant by exposure to low levels, it is suggested that naturally occurring tolerance may be achieved by acclimatization (Fraser 1980). Research is needed on Pb transformation mechanisms, on toxic forms of Pb and interaction effects with other compounds, and on effects of Pb-contaminated sediments on benthos (Wong et al. 1978).

AMPHIBIANS AND REPTILES

Lead poisoning in adult leopard frogs (*Rana pipiens*) is indicated by a series of signs: sloughing of integument; sluggishness; decreased muscle tone; decreases in red blood cells, white blood cells, neutrophils, and monocytes; erosion of the gastric mucosa; and (before death) excitement, salivation, and muscular twitching. The 30-day LC-50 value for *R. pipiens* was 105 mg Pb/l, but some deaths and elevated liver residues were noted at water concentrations as low as 25 mg/l (Kaplan et al. 1967). In soft water (99 mg CaCO$_3$/l) some marbled salamanders (*Ambystoma opacum*) exposed to 1.4 mg Pb/l died in 8 days (EPA 1985). At about 1.0 mg/l, Pb blocked synaptic transmission by competitive inhibition of calcium in the bullfrog, *Rana catesbeiana* (Kober and Cooper 1976). At 0.5 mg Pb/l, tadpoles of *Rana utricularia* required additional time to metamorphose; and at 1.5 mg Pb/l, thyroid histopathology was recorded and the delay in metamorphosis was more pronounced (Yeung 1978).

No data were available on toxic or sublethal effects of Pb to reptiles under controlled conditions.

BIRDS

Lead poisoning resulting from the ingestion of Pb shotgun pellets has been recognized as a cause of waterfowl deaths since the late 1800's (Wetmore 1919; Bellrose 1959). More than a million ducks--especially mallards--and geese die annually from Pb shot poisoning (Clemens et al. 1975). The principal cause is the ingestion of spent shot by migrating birds feeding in heavily hunted areas. The pellets are retrieved from the marshy bottoms of shallow and deep water by waterfowl in search of feed and grit. Shot retained in the gizzard is solubilized by a combination of the powerful muscular grinding action and the low pH (2.0 to 3.5) of gizzard contents. The released Pb is available for absorption, producing weakened birds whose reproductive abilities are reduced and that may starve or fall prey to predators (Clemens et al. 1975). Absorbed lead causes a variety of effects leading to death, including damage to the nervous system, muscular paralysis, inhibition of heme synthesis, and damage to kidneys and liver (Mudge 1983). Lead poisoning in waterfowl is a debilitating disease in which death follows exposure by an average of 2 to 3 weeks (Friend 1985). During this time, affected birds lose mobility, tend to avoid other birds, and become increasingly susceptible to predation and other causes of mortality. Accordingly, acute large-scale die-offs of Pb-poisoned waterfowl are uncommon (Friend 1985).

The relation between incidence of Pb shot in waterfowl gizzards and biological effects varies widely, and is probably a function of shot availability caused by differences in shooting intensity, size of pellets, availability of grit, firmness of soil and sediments, and depth of surface water (Street 1983). Also, Pb accumulations and the frequency of avian Pb toxicosis following ingestion of Pb shot are modified by the age and sex of the bird, geographic location, habitat, and time of year (Finley and Dieter 1978; Mudge 1983; Srebocan and Rattner 1988).

The effect of diet on vulnerability to Pb makes interpretation of published information on experimental Pb poisoning in waterfowl extremely difficult (Chasko et al. 1984). For example, many mallards on a diet of corn die within 10 to 14 days after ingesting a single Pb shot, whereas similar birds on a balanced commercial duck ration appear outwardly normal after ingesting as many as 32 pellets of the same size (Wobeser 1981). Also, multiple nutritional deficiencies may have additional effects in potentiating the toxicity of Pb in mallards (Carlson and Nielsen 1985).

Birds of prey may ingest Pb in the form of shot from dead or crippled game animals, or as biologically incorporated Pb from Pb-poisoned waterfowl, small roadside mammals, and invertebrates (Stendell 1980; Pattee 1984). Lead poisoning in carnivorous birds has been reported in various species of eagles, condors, vultures, and falcons, and most--if not all--cases seem to result from ingestion of Pb shot in food items (Custer et al. 1984). Some raptors ingest many shot in a short time. For example, the stomach of a bald eagle suspected of dying from Pb poisoning contained 75 shot (Jacobson et al. 1977). Results of experimental Pb shot poisoning of bald eagles (Table 7) confirmed results of nationwide monitoring showing that 5.4% of all dead eagles found in 1974-1975 died of Pb poisoning, as evidenced by liver Pb levels of 23 to 38 mg/kg fresh weight (Pattee et al. 1981). Ingestion of food containing biologically incorporated Pb, although contributing to the Pb burden of carnivorous birds, is unlikely in itself to cause clinical Pb poisoning (Custer et al. 1984). A similar case is made for powdered Pb (Franson et al. 1983), and forms of Pb other than shot (Table 7); the strong indication is that the form in which Pb is ingested is crucial.

Signs of Pb poisoning in birds have been extensively documented (Bellrose 1951, 1959; Jordan and Bellrose 1951; Clemens et al. 1975; Forbes and Sanderson 1978; Hunter and Wobeser 1980; Pattee et al. 1981; Wobeser 1981; Franson and Custer 1982; Johnson et al. 1982; Eastin et al. 1983; Kendall and Scanlon 1983; Street 1983; Di Giulio and Scanlon 1984; Fimreite 1984; Gjerstad and Hanssen 1984; Hudson et al. 1984; Anderson and Havera 1985; Burger and Gochfeld 1985; Carlson and Nielsen 1985; Friend 1985; Hoffman et al. 1985a; Lumeij 1985; Beyer et al. 1988). Outwardly, Pb-poisoned birds show the following signs: loss of appetite, lethargy, weakness, emaciation, tremors, drooped wings, green liquid feces, and impaired locomotion, balance, and depth perception. Internally, Pb-poisoned birds show microscopic lesions of the proventricular epithelium, pectoral muscles, brain, proximal tubular epithelium of the kidney, and bone medullary osteocytes; an enlarged bile-filled gall bladder; anemia; elevated protoporphyrin IX levels in blood; decreased ALAD activity levels in blood, brain, and liver; reduced brain weight; abnormal skeletal development; cephalic edema; and esophageal impaction. Postmortem examination of Pb-poisoned birds may show edematous lungs; serous fluid in the pleural cavity; bile regurgitation; abnormal gizzard lining; a usually pale, emaciated, and dehydrated carcass; and elevated Pb levels in liver (>2 mg/kg fresh weight, >10 mg/kg dry weight), kidney (>6 mg/kg dry weight), and blood (> 0.2 mg/1).

Toxic and sublethal effects of Pb and its compounds on birds held under controlled conditions vary widely with species, with age and sex, and with form and dose of administered Pb (Table 7). Several generalizations are possible: decreased blood ALAD and increased protoporphyrin IX activity levels are useful early indicators of Pb exposure; Pb shot and certain organolead compounds are the most toxic forms of Pb; nestlings are more sensitive than older stages; and tissue Pb concentrations and pathology both increase in birds given multiple doses over extended periods (Table 7).

Table 7. Lethal and sublethal effects of lead to selected species of birds.

Species, route of administration, dose, and other variables	Effects	Reference[a]
Northern pintail, *Anas acuta*		
Single oral dose of 2 No. 5 pellets	No difference from control group in band recovery rate from hunter kills	1
Mallard, *Anas platyrhynchos*		
Single oral dose of 1 No. 4 shot (1.4 g)	Some deaths. Residues (mg/kg fresh weight) >3 in brain, >10 in clotted heart blood, >6 in kidney, and up to 20 in liver	2
Single oral dose		
1 No. 6 shot (1.0 g)	Mortality 9% in 20 days	3
1 No. 4 shot (1.6 g)	Mortality 19% in 20 days	3
2 No. 6 shot (2.0 g)	Mortality 23% in 20 days	3
4 No. 6 shot (4.0 g)	Mortality 36% in 20 days	3
6 No. 6 shot (6.0 g)	Mortality 50% in 20 days	3
8 No. 6 shot (8.0 g)	Mortality 100% in 20 days	3
Single oral dose of 1 No. 4 shot (205 mg), equal to 151 mg/kg body weight (BW)	Some deaths; blood ALAD activity depressed 30% after 3 months, 15% after 4 months	4
Single oral dose of 1 No. 4 Pb shot (200 mg)	Residues (mg/kg dry weight femur) 488 in laying hen, 114 in nonlaying hen, and 9 in drake	5
Single oral dose of 1 shot (200 mg)	After 30 days, residues (mg/kg fresh weight) 1.0 in blood, 2.5 in liver, and 0.5 in brain. Decrease in ALAD activity in blood and cerebellum	6
Single oral dose of shot	Dosed birds recaptured in significantly greater numbers than controls	7
Single oral dose of tetraethyllead	LD-50 of 107 mg/kg BW. Signs of intoxication included	

	excessive drinking, regurgitation, hypoactivity, muscular incoordination, fluffed feathers, eyelid drooping, tremors, and loss of appetite. Regurgitation within 7 min, other signs as soon as 20 min, and death usually between 1 and 4 days posttreatment. Remission took up to 8 days	7a
Fed diets containing 25 mg Pb/kg, as lead nitrate, for 12 weeks	No deaths; no pathology; no significant accumulations of Pb in liver, kidney, or bone; no changes in hemoglobin or hematocrit; decrease in blood ALAD activity, and increase in blood Pb levels--both returned to normal diet within 3 weeks on Pb-free diet	8
Fed diets containing 100 mg Pb^{2+}/kg	Elevated levels in bone (9.6 mg/kg fresh weight vs. 0.7 in controls) and egg (1.3 vs. 0.9 in controls)	9
Fed diets containing metallic Pb for 42 days 100 mg/kg diet dry weight	Elevated Pb levels (mg/kg dry weight) in kidney (23), liver (7), and bone (5)	10
10 mg/kg diet	Residues (mg/kg dry weight) of 4 in kidney (vs. <0.5 in controls), 0.7 in liver (vs. <0.5 in controls), and 0.8 in bone (vs. 0.9 in controls)	10
Ducks, *Anas* spp. Single oral dose of 2 shot (254 mg) or 5 shot (635 mg)	Weight loss, emaciation, elevated Pb concentrations in bone, some deaths. American black duck, *Anas rubripes*, more sensitive than mallards	11
Birds Dietary route, 11 species,	All had inclusions in proximal	

diagnosed as Pb-poisoned	convoluted tubules of kidney; liver Pb residues ranged from 3.1 to 15 mg/kg fresh weight	12
Lethal dietary administration of lead acetate, 6 species	Before death, birds were emaciated and showed increases in blood protoporphyrin and decreases in ALAD; renal intra-nuclear inclusion bodies were present in 83% of all birds that died from Pb poisoning. Median Pb concentrations (mg/kg fresh weight) ranged in the liver from 20 in male red-winged blackbirds (*Agelaius phoeniceus*) to 111 in female northern bobwhites (*Colinus virginianus*), and in the kidney from 22 mg/kg in the blackbird to 190 in the bobwhite	13
Rock dove, *Columba livia*		
Intragastric administration of 6.25 mg Pb (as lead acetate)/kg BW daily for 64 weeks	Anemia, elevation of erythrocyte porphyrin, kidney pathology; residues (mg/kg fresh weight) of 603 in kidney, 501 in bone, 8 in liver, 2 in brain, 4.4 in blood, 0.8 in sciatic nerve, and 0.1 in crop	14
Intubation of 6.25 mg Pb (as lead acetate)/ kg BW, chronic exposure	Interfered with four-step learning sequence; elevated blood Pb levels remained for 5 weeks after Pb exposure	15
Japanese quail, *Coturnix japonica*		
Single oral dose of tetraethyllead	LD-50 of 24.6 mg/kg BW	7a
Fed diets containing different forms of Pb for 5 days		
5,000 mg metallic Pb/kg	No effect on survival or food consumption	16
5,000 mg Pb (as lead nitrate)/kg	No overt signs of toxicity	16
5,000 mg Pb (as lead subacetate $C_4H_{10}O_8Pb_3$)/kg	No overt signs of toxicity	16
2,761/mg Pb (as	LD-50	16

lead arsenate)/kg

Prairie falcon, *Falco mexicanus*

Fed shotgun-killed pheasants and ducks	Death, preceded by vomiting, ataxia, blindness, and convulsions. Lead shot recovered from stomach; residues (mg/kg dry weight) of 57 in liver and 78 in kidney	17

American kestrel, *Falco sparverius*

Fed mallard homogenate containing 16 to 87 (biologically incorporated) mg Pb/kg fresh weight for 60 days	Residues of 0.4 mg/kg fresh weight in liver and 7.6 mg/kg dry weight in bone	18
Oral administration of 1 No. 9 shot daily for 60 days	Residues (mg/kg fresh weight) of 0.4 in liver and 28.7 in bone	18
Fed control diet containing 0.4 mg Pb^{2+}/kg fresh weight	Residues of 0.1 mb/kg fresh weight in liver and 4.2 mg/kg dry weight in bone	18
Fed diets containing 50 mg metallic Pb powder/kg for at least 5 months	Blood ALAD reduced 80%; liver residues of 1.3 to 2.4 mg/kg dry weight; no effects on blood chemistry	19
As above, except diet contained 10 mg/kg	No measurable effects	19

Fed diets containing metallic Pb powder for 6 months

50 mg Pb/kg diet	No adverse effects on survival, egg laying, fertility, or egshell thickness. Elevated residues (mg/kg dry weight) in humerus (13), tibia (62), and liver (2)	20
10 mg Pb/kg diet	Elevated Pb in bone (4 to 9 mg/kg dry weight vs. <0.8 in controls) and in liver (3 vs. <0.5 in controls)	20

Nestlings dosed orally

with metallic Pb powder daily for 10 days		
625 mg/kg BW	Mortality (40% in 6 days); reduced growth; reduced kidney and liver weight; abnormal skeletal development; ALAD depression in all tissues examined; elevated burdens (mg/kg fresh weight) in kidney (15), liver (6), and brain (3)	21
125 mg/kg BW	Reduced growth, reduced brain weight, abnormal skeletal development, ALAD depressions in hematopoietic tissues, elevated burdens (mg/kg fresh weight) in kidney (7), and liver (4)	21
25 mg/kg BW	ALAD depression in all tissues examined; burdens (mg/kg fresh weight) elevated in kidney (3) and in liver 1.4)	21
Fed 60 days with homogenized cockerels (*Gallus* sp.) containing up to 448 mg (biologically incorporated) Pb/kg dry weight	No effect on survival, growth, hemoglobin, hematocrit, and erythrocyte number. Elevated burdens in kidney, liver, femur, brain, and blood	22
Chicken, *Gallus* sp.		
Fed diets containing 1,850 mg Pb/kg, as lead acetate, for 4 weeks	No deaths or severe clinical hematological effects; growth rate suppressed 47%, blood Pb residues 3.2 to 8.3 mg/L	23
Bald eagle, *Haliaeetus leucocephalus*		
Oral administration of 10 No. 4 shot (2,000 mg)		
Eagles dying 10 to 133 days posttreatment	Residue levels (mg/kg dry weight) 0.9 in muscle, 1.4 in brain, 6 in kidney, 10 in tibia, 10.3 in humerus, 10.4 in femur, and 16.6 in liver. Loss in body weight 16% to 23%	

	at death	24
Eagle sacrificed at day 133 posttreatment (bird went blind)	Residue levels (mg/kg dry weight) <0.1 in muscle, 2.1 in brain, 3.2 in kidney, 3.4 in liver, and 12.2 to 13.8 in bone	24
Controls	Residue levels (mg/kg dry weight) <0.1 muscle, 0.1 in brain, 0.4 in liver, 0.5 in kidney, and 4.5 to 6.6 in bone	24
Willow ptarmigan, *Lagopus lagopus*		
Single oral dose		
1 No. 6 shot (100 mg)	Weight loss of 12% in 15 days; residues of 3.3 mg/kg fresh weight in liver, 56 mg/kg dry weight in tibia	25, 26
3 No. 6 shot (300 mg)	Some deaths between days 8 and 15 posttreatment, reduced food intake, weight loss, lethargy, diarrhea; residues of 7.3 mg/kg fresh weight liver, 139 dry weight tibia	25, 26
6 No. 6 shot (600 mg)	If shot retained in gizzard, death resulted; residues (mg/kg) 72 fresh weight in liver, 154 dry weight in tibia	25, 26
Controls	Residues (mg/kg) 0.1 fresh weight in liver, 5 dry weight in tibia	25, 26
Raptors, 4 spp.		
Fed rock doves (*Columba livia*) and brown hares (*Lepus europaeus*) containing Pb shot for 3 weeks to 6 months	Death preceded by weight loss, convulsions, and inability to fly. Residues (mg/kg dry weight) at death ranged from 57 to 175 in liver, and 34 to 221 in kidney	27
Common tern, *Sterna hirundo*		
Single injection of 200 mg Pb^{2+}	Adverse effects on behavior (locomotion, balance, righting response, feeding tasks, behavioral thermo-regulation); most apparent	

| | within 5 days postinjection | 28 |

Ringed turtle-dove, *Streptopelia risoria*

Single oral dose of 2 pellets (220 mg)	Blood Pb (mg/L) 4.69 at 24 h, and 0.14 at 14 days (vs. control values of 0.004 to 0.012 mg/L); blood ALAD depressed from 24 h through 14 days	29
Single oral dose of 4 shot (440 mg)	Mortality 71% at 6 □C in 7 days; nil at 21 □C in 9 days--but some with seizures and kidney histopathology. No spermatozoa in seminiferous tubules. Lead residues elevated in bone, liver, and brain in both groups, but more elevated in cold-stressed group	30, 31
Single oral dose of 4 shot (440 mg)	Testicular damage in adults held at 6 □C or 21 °C; mortality higher in cold-stressed group	32
Single oral dose of 4 shot (488 mg)	Some deaths. Intranuclear inclusion bodies in cells of kidney proximal convoluted tubules	12
Single oral dose of 75 mg Pb/kg BW, as lead acetate	Some deaths; kidney damage	12
Intubation with 75 mg Pb (as lead acetate)/kg BW daily for 7 days	Residues, (mg/kg dry weight) 457 in kidney, 29 in liver, and 12.4 in brain; seizures; depressed blood ALAD activity; blood Pb concentration 311 mg/L	33
Controls	Concentrations (mg/kg dry weight) 8.2 in kidney, 3.0 in brain, 1.2 in liver; blood Pb concentration 18 mg/L	33
Drinking water with 100 µg Pb^{2+}/L for 2 weeks before pairing, and throughout a breeding cycle	Reduction in testes weight and speratozoa number. No effect on egg production or fertility. Bone Pb levels higher than controls especially in females. Significantly higher Pb	

	concentrations in bone, liver, and feather in progeny of Pb-treated parents than in controls	34
European starling, *Sturnus vulgaris*		
Oral administration (capsule) of triethyllead chloride at 2,000 ug daily (28 mg/kg BW) for 11 days, or until death	Mortality 100% by day 6. Dying birds showed decreased respiration, squatting, fluffed feathers, and abnormal head posture. Average residues (mg/kg fresh weight) 6.0 in bone, 7.3 in brain 19.9 in kidney, 20.0 in muscle, and 40.2 in liver.	35
As above, but dose was 200 ug daily (2.8 mg/kg BW)	No deaths, reduced food consumption. All tissue residues <2.0 mg/kg fresh weight (vs. <0.1 in controls).	35
Oral administration (capsule) of trimethyllead chloride at 2,000 ug daily (28 mg/kg BW) for 11 days, or until death	Mortality 100% by day 6. Signs included impaired balance, tremors, fluffed feathers, uncoordinated feeding movements, weight loss, inability to fly. Residues (mg/kg fresh weight) averaged 4.3 in bone, 11.0 in muscle, 16.7 in brain, 30.2 in kidney, and 82.4 in liver	35
As above, but dose was 200 µg daily (2.8 mg/kg BW)	No deaths, survivors hyperactive. Average tissue residues (mg/kg fresh weight) 0.4 in bone, 3.1 in muscle, 3.5 in brain, 3.7 in liver, and 5.4 in kidney	35
Mourning dove, *Zenaida macroura* Single oral dose		
1 No. 8 shot (72 mg)	Mortality 24% in 4 weeks; normal courtship and reproductive activities, but egg hatching significantly reduced; Pb residues elevated in kidney, liver, and bone	36
2 No. 8 shot (144 mg)	Mortality 60% in 4 weeks	36

61

4 No. 8 shot (288 mg)	Mortality 52% in 4 weeks	36
Single oral dose of		
4 No. 8 shot		
4 days posttreatment	Residues (mg/kg dry weight)	
	345 to 639 in kidney and	
	58 to 215 in liver (vs. <12 in	
	controls)	37
8 days posttreatment	Residues (mg/kg dry weight)	
	1,279 to 1,901 in kidney and	
	179 to 267 in liver	37

aReferences: 1, Deuel 1985; 2, Longcore et al. 1974a; 3, Longcore et al. 1974b; 4, Dieter and Finley 1978; 5, Finley and Dieter 1978; 6, Dieter and Finley 1979; 7, Bellrose 1951; 7a, Hudson et al. 1984; 8, Finley et al. 1976; 9, Haegele et al. 1974; 10, Di Giulio and Scanlon 1984; 11, Chasko et al. 1984; 12, Kendall and Scanlon 1985; 13, Beyer et al. 1988; 14, Anders et al. 1982; 15, Dietz et al. 1979; 16, Hill and Camardese 1986; 17, Redig et al. 1980; 18, Stendell 1980; 19, Franson et al. 1983; 20, Pattee 1984; 21, Hoffman et al. 1984a,b; 22, Custer et al. 1984; 23, Franson and Custer 1982; 24, Pattee et al. 1981; 25, Gjerstad and Hanssen 1984; 26, Fimreite 1984; 27, Macdonald et al. 1983; 28, Burger and Gochfeld 1985; 29, Kendall et al. 1982; 30, Kendall and Scanlon 1981; 31, Kendall and Scanlon 1984; 32, Veit et al. 1983; 33, Kendall and Scanlon 1982; 34, Kendall and Scanlon 1981; 35, Osborn et al. 1983; 36, Buerger et al. 1986; 37, Kendall and Scanlon 1983.

Trialkyllead salts are 10 to 100X more toxic to birds than are inorganic Pb salts; they tend to accumulate in lipophilic soft tissues in the yolk and developing embryo, and have high potential as neurotoxicants (Forsyth et al. 1985); accordingly more research is needed on alkyllead toxicokinetics. Some alkyllead compounds have been implicated in bird kills. In autumn 1979, about 2,400 birds of many species were found dead or disabled on the Mersey estuary, England, an important waterfowl and marsh bird wintering area; smaller kills were observed in 1980 and 1981 (Bull et al. 1983). Affected birds contained elevated Pb concentrations in liver (>7.5 mg/kg fresh weight), mostly as organolead. Bull et al. (1983) suggested that trialkyllead compounds were discharged from a petrochemical factory producing alkylleads, into the estuary where they were accumulated (up to 1.0 mg/kg fresh weight) by clams (*Macoma balthica*) and other invertebrates on which the birds could feed. Birds dosed experimentally with trialkyllead compounds died with the same behavioral and internal signs found in Mersey casualties; tissue levels of trialkyllead were similar in the two groups of birds (Osborn et al. 1983). Sublethal effects that might influence survival in the wild were found in both sublethally dosed and apparently healthy wild birds when tissue levels of trialkyllead compounds were matched in the two groups of birds. It was concluded that trialkyllead compounds were the main cause of the observed mortalities and that many apparently healthy birds were still at risk (Osborn et al. 1983).

Nestlings of altricial species (those confined to the nest for some time after hatch) may be considerably more sensitive to Pb exposure than adults, and also more sensitive than hatchlings of many precocial species (Hoffman et al. 1985a). Hatchlings of precocial species, including chickens, Japanese quail (*Coturnix coturnix*), mallards, and pheasants, are relatively tolerant to moderate Pb exposure, i.e., there was no effect on growth at dietary levels of 500 mg Pb/kg, or survival at 2,000 mg Pb/kg (Hoffman et al. 1985a,b).

Some species of domestic birds are resistant to Pb toxicosis. for example, blood Pb levels of 3.2 to 3.8 mg/l in Pb-stressed cockerels (*Gallus* sp.) were much higher than residues considered diagnostic for Pb poisoning in most domestic mammals, except swine--which tolerated up to 143 mg Pb/1 blood (Franson and Custer 1982).

MAMMALS

Three stages of recognizable Pb poisoning, or plumbism, have been reported in humans (NRCC 1973): (1) mild or severe dysfunction of the alimentary tract as shown by loss of appetite, constipation, abdominal cramps, headaches, general weakness, and fatigue; (2) atrophy of forearm extensor muscles., or paralysis of these muscles and more striking atrophy; and (3) lead encephalopathy, which occurs frequently in Pb-poisoned infants and young children, but only rarely in industrial workers. In general, people with hepatitis, anemia, and nervous disorders were more susceptible to Pb poisoning (Barth et al. 1973). The transfer of Pb across the human placenta and its potential threat to the fetus have been recognized for more than 100 years; women occupationally exposed to Pb showed a comparatively high abortion rate (Tachon et al. 1983). Sensitivity of the brain to the toxic effects of Pb is considerably greater in the fetus than in the infant or young child (EPA 1980). Lead is not considered carcinogenic to humans (Tsuchiya 1979). However, reports of chromosomal aberrations in human blood lymphocytes (Barth et al. 1973) suggested that Pb is a probable mutagen.

Signs of plumbism in domestic and laboratory animals (data on feral mammals are noticeably lacking), which are similar to those in humans, have been well documented (Barth et al. 1973; NRCC 1973; Mierau and Favara 1975; Davies et al. 1976; Roberts et al. 1976; Forbes and Sanderson 1978; Nriagu 1978b; Osweiler and Van Gelder 1978; Tsuchiya 1979; Ward and Brooks 1979; EPA 1980; Mahaffey et al. 1980; Hamir 1981; Harrison and Laxen 1981; Burrows and Borchard 1982; Demayo et al. 1982; Hamir et al. 1982; Mykkanen et al. 1982; Tachon et al. 1983; Gietzen and Wooley 1984; Berglind et al. 1985; Table 8). There is general agreement on several details: significant differences occur between species in response to Pb insult; effects of lead are more pronounced with organolead than inorganic lead compounds; younger developmental stages are the most sensitive; and the effects are exacerbated by elevated temperatures, and by diets deficient in minerals, fats, and proteins. Tetramethyllead, for example, is about 7X more toxic than tetraethyllead to animals, and both compounds showed toxic effects earlier than did inorganic Pb compounds. In severe cases, death is usually preceded by impairment of normal functions of the central nervous system, the gastrointestinal tract, and the muscular and hematopoietic systems. Signs include vomiting, lassitude, loss of appetite, uncoordinated body movements, convulsions, stupor, and coma. In nonfatal cases, signs may include depression, anorexia, colic, disturbed sleep patterns, diarrhea, anemia, visual impairment, blindness, susceptibility to bacterial infections, excessive salivation, eye blinking, renal malfunction, peripheral nerve diseases affecting the motor nerves of the extremities, reduced growth, reduced life span, abnormal social behavior, and learning impairment. Lead crosses the placenta and is passed in milk, producing early intoxication of the fetus during pregnancy and the newborn during lactation. High Pb doses in mammals induce abortion, reduce or terminate pregnancy, or can result in stillbirths or an increase in skeletal malformations. These signs, together with Pb levels in blood and tissues and histopathological examination, are used to diagnose Pb poisoning.

Lead adversely affected the survival of sensitive mammals tested at different concentrations (Table 8): 5 to 108 mg Pb/kg BW in rats (acute oral),0.32 mg Pb/kg BW daily in dogs (chronic oral), and 1.7 mg Pb/kg diet in horses (chronic dietary). Adverse sublethal effects (Table 8) were noted in monkeys given 0.1 mg Pb/kg BW daily (impaired learning 2 years postadministration) or fed diets containing 0.5 mg Pb/kg (abnormal social behavior); in rabbits given 0.005 mg Pb/kg BW (reduced blood ALAD activity) or 0.03 mg Pb/kg BW (elevated blood Pb levels); in mice at 0.05 mg Pb/kg BW (reduced ALAD activity); or in sheep at 0.05 mg Pb/kg BW (tissue accumulations).

Table 8. Lethal and sublethal effects of lead to selected species of mammals.

Species, dose, and other variables	Effects	Reference[a]
Cattle, cows, *Bos* spp.		
Tissue Pb (mg/kg fresh weight) 0.81 in blood, 26.4 in liver, 50.3 in kidney, and 400 in rumen contents	Signs of clinical Pb toxicosis observed	1
Calves given 2.7 mg Pb/kg body weight (BW), as Pb acetate, for 20 days; milk diet	Death	2
Calves given 3.0 to 3.5 mg Pb/kg BW daily for 3 months;	No effect	2

63

grain and hay diet		
Calves given 5 mg Pb/kg BW, as Pb acetate, for 7 days; grain and hay diet	Appeared normal	3
Calves given 5 mg Pb/kg BW, as Pb acetate, for 7 days; milk diet	Signes of Pb poisoning; some deaths	3,4
Calves given 5 mg Pb/kg BW daily for 10 to 20 days	Blindness, 16% mortality	4
Calves given forage containing 5 to 6 mg Pb/kg	Fatal in 2 months	1
Calves given 5 to 6 mg Pb/kg BW daily for 3 years	Chronic toxicity	2
Adults given 6 mg Pb/kg BW daily for 3 years	No deaths	5
Calves given 6 to 7 mg Pb/kg BW daily for 2 months	Fatal	2
Fed 6 to 7 mg Pb (as Pb acetate)/kg BW daily	Intoxication within 8 weeks; most dead at day 105	6
Consumed vegetation (17 to 20 mg Pb/kg fresh weight) near Pb battery recycling plant	Some deaths, mostly younger animals; neurological signs. Lead levels, in mg/kg fresh weight, were 13.8 to 35.8 in blood, 6.9 to 96.5 in feces, 97 in liver, and 138 in kidney. Histopathology of liver and kidney	7
Calves given 20 mg Pb/kg BW daily	Fatal in 8 to 22 days	2
Accidentally exposed for 10 days to toxic levels of Pb, as Pb shot, through corn silage. Silage storage area received shot from a nearby trap shooting range. Silage contained 32 mg Pb/kg	1.5% dead (2/70), 27% with signs of poisoning (kidney pathology, hemorrhaging). Tissue Pb concentrations of 16 mg/kg fresh weight in liver, >32 in kidney, and up to 0.8 in blood	6
Calves, single oral dose of 220 to 400 mg Pb/kg BW, as Pb acetate	LD-50	2
Total dose of 50 to 100 grams	Toxic	6
Dog, *Canis familiaris*		
Fed 0.32 mg Pb/kg BW daily	Chronic toxic level	4
Fed 3 mg Pb/kg BW daily, as	Anorexia and convulsions	

lead carbonate	at 180 days	8
Fed low calcium/phosphorus diet containing 100 mg Pb/kg, equivalent to about 3.5 mg Pb/kg BW	At 12 weeks, anemia, weight loss, and renal necrosis Tissue Pb levels (mg/kg fresh weight) 1.2 in brain, 1.7 in blood, 15.7 in spleen, 23.4 in liver, 32.2 in kidney, and 735 in bone	9
Total dose of 10 to 25 grams	Toxic	6
Goat, *Capra* sp.		
Total dose of 20 to 25 grams	Toxic	6
Guinea pig, *Cavia cobaya*		
Single intraperitoneal injection of 25 mg/kg BW, as Pb acetate	Reduced brain weight of newborn pigs. Effect synergized when dams were exposed to elevated (42 □C) temperatures for 24 h: 88% with microencephaly vs. 5% in group given 25 mg/kg without hyperthermia	10
Horse, *Equus caballus*		
Tissue Pb levels, in mg/kg fresh weight, of 0.39 in blood, 18 in liver, and 16 in kidney	Signs of clinical Pb toxicosis observed	1
Ate forage containing 1.7 mg Pb/kg	Fatal in several months	1
Consumed 2.4 mg Pb/kg BW daily	Lethal	4
Fed 6.25 mg Pb/kg BW daily for 105 days, as Pb acetate	No deaths; blood Pb levels of 350 to 380 µg/L at day 105	6
Fed hay collected near Idaho smelter containing 423 mg Pb/kg, equivalent to about 7.4 mg Pb/kg BW daily	All dead in 84 to 100 days. Total Pb ingested ranged from 136 to 154 grams	11
Fed 9.8 mg Pb/kg BW daily for 105 days, as Pb acetate	No deaths; blood Pb levels of 530 to 650 µg/L at day 105	6
Fed noncontaminated hay plus 10 mg Pg/kg BW daily, as Pb acetate	All dead in 113 to 304 days. Total Pb ingested ranged from 190 to 544 grams	11
Total dose of 500 to	Toxic	6

700 grams

Cat, *Felis domesticus*

Fed pine voles (*Pitymys pinetorium*) from orchard sprayed with Pb arsenate. Concentrations (mg Pb/kg dry weight) were 60.3 in whole voles, 5.7 in cat diet containing voles, and 3.2 in control cat diet	After 86 days, tissue residues elevated in cat kidney (1.3 mg Pb/kg dry weight vs. 0.2 for controls), liver (0.5 vs. 0.1), and bone (5.0 vs. 0.9)	12

Rabbit, *Lepus* sp.

Given 0.9, 0.03, 0.06, 0.15, 0.3, or 3 mg Pb/kg BW for 6 days	Blood Pb levels (µg/L) generally increased from 170 (control) to 910 (0.03), 530 (0.06), 1,430 (0.15), 1,930 (0.3), and 5,160 (3.0)	13
Exposed to 2.46 µg Pb/m³ air for life	No effect	13
>5 µg Pg/kg BW daily	Reduced blood ALAD activity	13

Mouse, *Mus* sp.

0.05 to 0.1 mg Pb/kg BW daily	Irreversible inhibition of ALAD activity in bone marrow and red blood cells	14
Tissue concentrations of 0.78 mg/kg femur bone marrow, 3.7 mg/L blood, 15.8 mg/kg brain, or 43 mg/kg liver	Inhibition of ALAD activity 50% within 10 min	14
1.5 mg Pb/kg BW daily, as tetraethyllead chloride	Reduction in success of implanted ova	8
2.2 mg/kg BW or 3 mg/kg BW daily, as tetraethyllead	Frequency of pregnancy reduced when dose given 3 to 5 days after mating	8
Pregnant females given single intrauterine injection of 20 mg Pb/kg BW on day 8 of gestation	Smaller litters, increased fetal deaths	15
800 mg Pb/L, as lead acetate, in drinking water for 11 weeks	Decrease in litter size, decreased survival of pups, and decrease birth weight	16
1,000 mg Pb/L in drinking water for 9 months	No effect on survival or fertility	4

Sheep, *Ovis aries*

Lambs fed 50 µg Pb/kg daily (~ 3 mg)	Tissue accumulations	5
Lambs exposed to low levels (350 µg Pb/L blood) *in utero*	Impaired visual discrimination and learning behavior	17
1.0 mg Pb/kg BW daily, as Pb acetate, for 3 months	Of 10 ewes, 3 aborted, 6 delivered normally, and 1 died; placental transfer of Pb established	5
Pregnant ewes given 3 mg Pb/kg BW daily	No effect	4
4.2 mg Pb/kg BW in diet for 4 weeks before gestation, and throughout gestation and lactation	Lambs showed impaired learning	18
Fed 5 mg Pb/kg BW first 45 days of pregnancy	Bore normal full-term lambs	9
Given 5 mg Pb/kg BW daily for one year	No adverse effects	5
Pregnant ewes given 5.7 mg Pb/kg BW daily	Fatal	4
Nonpregnant ewes given 6 mg Pb/kg BW daily	Toxic threshold	4
8 mg Pb/kg BW daily for 220 days	Mortality	5
Fed 9 mg Pb/kg BW throughout pregnancy	Aborted and died	9
Fed diet containing 138 mg/kg dry weight for 124 days	Elevated residues in bone (22 mg/kg vs. 2.6 in controls) and kidney (8.3 vs. 1.0)	4
Lambs fed diets containing 400 mg Pb/kg, but deficient in calcium and sulphate	Dead within 5 weeks	4
Lambs fed diets containing 400 mg Pb/kg, diet adequate in minerals	Some weight loss in 10 months, but normal otherwise	4
Single oral dose of 600 mg Pb/kg BW	Fatal	9
Total dose of 20 to 25 grams	Toxic	6

Primates, various species

Cynmolgus monkey, *Macaca iris*

Intramuscular injection of 1.0 mg Pb/kg BW daily during pregnancy or lactation	Fetus exposed to lead through placenta or maternal milk	19

1.5 mg Pb/L in drinking water as lead acetate, for 9 months (equivalent to 0.5 mg Pb/kg BW daily), or 6 mg/L (2 mg/kg BW), or 15 mg/L (5 mg/kg BW)	Increasing blood Pb levels from third month, according to dose; kidney pathology. Effects more severe in animals on low calcium diets	20
Intramuscular administration of 5 mg Pb^{2+}/kg BW daily during pregnancy or lactation	Abortions and death in pregnant monkeys; cerebral pathology in newborns	19
Cynmolgus monkey, *Macaca fascicularis*		
Dosed orally from birth to age 200 days with 100 µg Pb (as Pb acetate)/kg BW, 5x weekly, milk substitute diet	Blood Pb concentration of 254 µg/L; declined to 131 µg/L over next 100 to 150 days. At age 3 years, impaired ability to perform motor discrimination reversal tasks	21
As above, except dose is 50 µg Pb/kg BW	Blood Pb levels of 154 µg/L (vs. 35 µg/L in controls), declining to 109 µg/L at day 150 post-administration. At age 3 years, group showed impaired color discrimination. No overt signs of toxicity, normal blood chemistry (except Pb), normal growth and development skills	21
Rhesus monkey, *Macaca mulatta*		
Infants given 0.5 mg Pg/kg diet for 4 weeks	Hyperactivity, insomnia, abnormal social behavior	18
Adults given 20 mg Pb/L in drinking water for 4 weeks	No effect	18
Baboon, *Papio anubis*		
Intratracheal injection of lead carbonate at doses of 50 to 135 mg Pb/kg BW for 29 to 362 days	73% dead (11/15) on receiving total dose of 1,250 to 7,800 mg Pb. Before death, some animals lost weight, became increasingly aggressive, had hepatic centrilobular necrosis, were uncoordinated and weak, and experienced convulsions; the blood contained up to 62 mg Pb/L	22
Single injection of 105 mg Pb/kg BW	Blood Pb concentrations rose from 117 µg/L at start to 3,100 µg/L at day 4 postadministration;	

	blood Pb remained >1,000 µg/L	
	for at least 24 days	22
Rat, *Rattus* spp.		
Exposed to 10 µg Pb/m^3	Elevated tissue residues in	
air for one year	blood, soft tissues, and bone	13
Exposed to 21.5 µg Pb/m^3	Blood Pb increased, but stabilized	
air for one year	after 4 months; Pb levels remained	
	elevated in bone, kidney, and	
	liver after 6 months	13
1.5 mg Pb/L in drinking water	Disturbed sleep patterns	18
for several days		
Weanling females given 0.0,	At 25 mg/L and higher, growth	
0.5, 5, 25, 50, or 250	retardation and delayed vaginal	
mg Pb (as Pb acetate)/L	opening observed; some maternal	
drinking water for 6 to 7	deaths occurred and were	
weeks, then mated and exposed	associate with blood Pb	
continuously through gestation	concentrations >200 µg/L.	
and lactation	Some pup malformations and	
	deaths in all groups. The	
	5 mg/L group had elevated	
	blood Pb levels	23
Single intravenous injection		
(mg Pb/kg BW in parentheses)		
Tetramethyllead (80)	LD-50	24
Tetraethyllead (10)	LD-50	24
Trimethyllead (20 to 25)	LD-50	24
Triethyllead (8)	LD-50	24
Single oral dose (mg Pb/kg BW)		
Tetramethyllead (108)	LD-50	24
Tetraethyllead (12)	LD-50	24
Single intraperitoneal		
injection (mg Pb/kg BW)		
Tetramethyllead (70 to 100)	LD-50	24
Tetraethyllead (10)	LD-50	24
Trimethyllead (17)	LD-50	24
Triethyllead (5)	LD-50	24
5 mg Pb/L drinking water,	Lowered survival and	
lifetime exposure	reduced longevity	4
Single intraperitoneal	Depressed food intake, and	
injection of 7 mg Pb/kg BW,	hyperactivity	25
as tetraethyllead		
Male weanlings exposed to age	At day 86: behavioral deficits;	

50 days to drinking water containing 25 mg Pg/L, as Pb acetate	blood Pb concentrations of 150 to 200 µg/L; brain Pb levels (µg/kg) 70 in treated group vs. 28 in controls	26
25 mg Pb/kg diet for 3 weeks	Increased locomotor activity	18
21-day-old rats exposed to 50, 100, or 500 mg Pb/L drinking water, as Pb acetate, for 335 days	Impaired behavior during first 4 months at 50 mg/L, but not thereafter. At 100 mg Pb/L and higher, behavior was impaired for at least 100 days postadministration. Brain and blood Pb levels reflected exposure concentration and duration	27
Neonatal rats given 50 mg Pb/kg BW intragastrically as Pb acetate, on days 6 to 18 postpartum	Impaired transfer of maze learning acquired during food deprivation	28
100 mg/kg BW daily, as lead nitrate	Some deaths of progeny in 3 weeks	8
Lead acetate in drinking water at 100, and 300 mg Pb/L from age 21 to 55 days	Impaired motor skills	29
200 mg/kg BW daily	50% of progeny dead in 3 weeks	8
4,000 mg Pb/L in drinking water for 130 days	Serum testosterone levels depressed, Leydig cell lesions; no effect at lower concentration tested (2,000 mg/L)	30
Nursing rats given diets containing zero, 2,000, 4,000, or 10,000 mg Pb/kg as metallic Pb powder	Lead-treated rats showed dose-related response to noise stimuli. Blood Pb levels (µg/L) in pups were 40 for controls, 250 for the 2,000 mg/kg group, 360 for the 4,000 mg/kg group, and 550 for the 10,000 mg/kg group	31
Swine, *Sus* sp.		
Oral doses of 64 mg Pb/kg BW, as Pb acetate, 6x weekly for 13 weeks	No deaths, reduced blood ALAD activity, blood Pb concentration (a remarkable) 143 mg/L	32
As above, except doses administered intraperitoneally	All died	32
Total dose of 10 to 25 grams	Toxic	6

a References: 1, Osweiler and Van Gelder 1983; 2, Zmudzki et al. 1983; 3, Zmudzki et al. 1984; 4, Demayo et al. 1982; 5, NRCC 1973; 6, Dollahite et al. 1978; 7, Kwatra et al. 1986; 8, Clark 1979; 9, Forbes and Sanderson 1978; 10, Edwards and Beatson 1984; 11, Burrows and Borchard 1982; 12, Gilmartin et al. 1985; 13, Barth et al. 1973; 14, Schlick et al. 1983; 15, Wide 1985; 16, Sharma and Kanwar 1985; 17, EPA 1980; 18, Nriagu 1978b; 19, Tachon et al. 1983; 20, Colle et al. 1980; 21, Rice 1985; 22, Hopkins 1970; 23, Kimmel et al. 1980; 24, Branica and Konrad 1980; 25, Czech and Hoium 1984; 26, Cory-Slechta et al. 1985; 27, Cory-Slechta et al. 1983; 28, Massaro et al. 1986; 29, Cory-Slechta et al. 1981; 30, Zirkin et al. 1985; 31, Barrett and Livesey 1985; 32, Lassen and Buck 1979.

Although Pb is undeniably toxic at high levels of exposure, the implications of lower levels of exposure are poorly defined (Nriagu 1978b). Behavioral effects such as hyperactivity, distractability, and decreased learning ability, as well as certain peripheral neuropathies, have been ascribed to subclinical Pb exposure (Hejtmancik et al. 1982). Impaired learning ability of Pb-stressed animals showing no obvious signs of Pb intoxication has been documented for rats (Cory-Slechta et al. 1981, 1983, 1985; Angell and Weiss 1982; Nation et al. 1982; Geist et al. 1985; Massaro et al. 1986), sheep (Nriagu 1978b; EPA 1980), and primates (Rice 1985)--although variability was great in all studies. Some learning deficits may be reversible and may not persist beyond a period of rehabilitation (Geist et al. 1985), and some may be induced only at relatively high exposure levels (Hastings et al. 1984). Abnormal social behavior (usually aggression) has been reported in baboons and monkeys (Hopkins 1970; Nriagu 1978b), although mice showed inhibited development of isolation-induced aggression (Ogilvie and Martin 1982). Altered parent-child relationships were suggested when suckling rats were used as surrogates. In that study, pregnant rats fed diets containing powdered Pb nursed for longer periods than normal, and the resultant offspring were slower to explore their environment (Barrett and Livesey 1983). Lead-exposed pups, with blood Pb levels as low as 200 ug/l (considered elevated but within the "normal" range) at weaning, showed an altered dam-pup interaction that resulted in the dam spending longer periods in the nest than usual. Retarded development of Pb-treated pups may account for the longer bouts of nesting by Pb-stressed dams, and the delay in age at which pups explore and learn. Barrett and Livesey (1983) concluded that maternal behavior was related to delays in pup development, and that the functional isolation of pups from their environment may be the antecedent to altered behavior later in maturity.

No data are currently available on effects of Pb-induced altered parent-offspring relationships, impaired learning ability, or abnormal social behavior for any population of free-ranging wildlife.

Ingestion of Pb-containing paint from bars or walls is a significant cause of death among captive wild animals--including many species of apes, monkeys, bears, ferrets, pinnipeds, foxes, panthers, bats, raccoons, and armadillos--and is probably underreported (Hopkins 1970; Zook et al. 1972; Fowler 1975; Forbes and Sanderson 1978). A similar situation exists for domestic animals--including dogs, cats, goats, horses, swine, cattle, and sheep (Dollahite et al. 1978; Forbes and Sanderson 1978; Osweiler and Van Gelder 1978; Hamir 1981). Passage of laws regulating the amount of Pb in paint has decreased the frequency of Pb poisoning, but many animals are still at risk from this source. Lead also occurs in used motor oils, gasoline, batteries, shot, putty, golf balls, linoleum, and printers ink--all of which are considered sources of Pb poisoning to domestic animals (Dollahite et al. 1978).

Although the use of lead arsenate as an insecticide in orchards is diminishing, residues of Pb still remain in the upper soil surface and will continue to remain bioavailable almost indefinitely (Gilmartin et al. 1985).

Naturally occurring radiolead-210, which has a half-life of 22 years, is a significant contributor to the natural radiation dose in man; comparatively high levels have been reported in certain grasses and lichens, and their consumers, such as reindeer, caribou, and ptarmigan, as well as in lanternfishes (Nriagu 1978b). The implications of this finding to wildlife health are unknown.

CURRENT RECOMMENDATIONS

Proposed Pb criteria for the protection of natural resources and human health are numerous and disparate (Table 9). Some of the criteria do not provide adequate protection. The most recent criteria for aquatic life protection, for example, range from 1.3 to 7.7 ug total waterborne Pb/1 (Table 9; EPA 1985); however, within this range high accumulations and adverse effects on growth and reproduction were recorded among sensitive species. Moreover, certain organolead compounds were lethal to some species of aquatic biota within this range, but no criteria have been formulated yet for this highly toxic group of chemicals. Nor have any criteria been proposed for Pb in tissues of aquatic biota connoting elevated or hazardous levels to the organism. It is noteworthy that health effects to man through ingestion of Pb-contaminated seafood (and probably other fishery products) are considered negligible. Total Pb concentrations observed in highly polluted areas in the 1970's were usually about one-tenth those showing effects on marine organisms (Branica and Konrad 1980).

Organolead compounds are more toxic than ionic forms. Since methylation of ionic Pb in vivo or in stored tissues is possible, and since some liver enzyme systems are capable of converting tetraethyllead to the more toxic triethyllead species, it would appear that the current Canadian permissible concentration limit of 10 mg Pb/kg fresh weight in fishery products should be reevaluated downwards (Sirota and lithe 1977). Downward evaluation has also been recommended for the standard of 2 mg/kg in the UK, where new guidelines have been recommended for total Pb and for tetralkyllead compounds in fishery products (Wong et al. 1981). Increasing use of organolead compounds as wood preservatives, as biocides, and as catalysts in the manufacture of plastics, polyurethanes, and polyvinyl chlorides (Walsh and Tilson 1984) may adversely affect survival, sensory reponsiveness, and behavioral reactivity in aquatic organisms (Chau et al. 1980; Maddock and Taylor 1980; Wong et al. 1981; Demayo et al. 1982) and avian wildlife (Bull et al. 1983; Osborn et al. 1983; Forsyth et al. 1985). It seems that additional research is needed on organolead toxicokinetics, with special reference to fishery and wildlife resources.

Table 9. Proposed lead criteria for the protection of natural resources and human health.

Resource, (units), and other variables	Criterion	Reference[a]
Crops		
Irrigation water (mg/L)		
USA		
Neutral and alkaline soils	<10	Demayo et
Acidic soils	<5	al. 1982
Chronic use	<5	Abbasi and
Short-term use	<20	Soni 1986
Canada		
Continuous use	<5	Demayo et
Intermittent use	<10	al. 1982
Australia		
Aquatic life		
Freshwater (μg total Pb/L)		
USA		
Water hardness, in mg $CaCO_3$/L		
50	1.3[b], 34[c]	EPA 1985
100	3.2[b], 82[c]	
200	7.7[b], 200[c]	
Great Lakes		
Superior	<100	Harrison and
Huron	<200	Laxen 1981
Others	<250	
England	<400	

Seawater (µg total Pb/L)	5.6[b], 140[c]	EPA 1985
Water (µg/L)		
Tetraalkyllead	<1	Maddock and
Trialkyllead	<100	Taylor 190
Sewage effluent limits (µg/L)		
California	<4,000	Harrison and
Industrial discharge limits		Laxen 1981
to surface waters (µg/L)		
Illinois	<100	
USA	<500	
Canada	<2,000	
Switzerland	<5,000	
Birds		
Canvasback, *Aythya valisineria*		
Elevated		
Wingbones, immatures		
(mg/kg dry weight)	>20	Fleming 1981
Blood (mg/L)	>0.2	Dieter et al. 1976
American kestrel, *Falco sparverius*		
Nestlings (mg/kg fresh weight)		
Elevated		
Liver	>2	Hoffman et al.
Kidney	>6	1985a
Poisoned		
Liver	>5	
Kidney	>15	
Bald eagle,		
Haliaeetus leucocephalus		
Elevated (mg/kg dry weight)		
Kidney	>6	Pattee et al.
Liver	>10	1981
Waterfowl		
Elevated (mg/kg dry weight)		
Liver	>2	Friend 1985
Blood	>0.2	
Poisoned (mg/kg fresh weight)		
Liver		
Total Pb	>8	
Trimethyllead	>0.5	Osborn et al. 1983
Blood	>0.4	Birkhead 1983
Mammals		
Cattle, *Bos* spp.		

Poisoned (mg/kg fresh weight)		
Blood	>1	Kwatra et al.
Liver	>20	1986
Kidney	>40	
Feces	>35	
Domestic livestock		
Drinking water (µg/L)		
USA	<100	Demayo et al.
Australia	<250	1982
Canada		
Horse	<500	
Others	<1,000	
Forage (mg/kg fresh weight)		
Horse	<80	Edwards and
Cattle	<200	Clay 1977
Tissue residues		
Unstressed (mg/kg fresh weight)		
Blood	<0.2	Osweiler and
Liver	<1.1	Van Gelder 1978
Kidney	<1.2	
Mouse, *Mus* sp.		
Elevated (mg/kg body weight daily)		
Total intake	>0.05	Schlick et al. 1983
Mule deer, *Odocoileus hemionus*		
Excessive (mg/day)		
Total intake	>3	Harrison and Dyer
1984		
Raccoon, *Procyon lotor*		
Elevated (mg/kg fresh weight)		
Liver	>10	Diters and
		Nielsen 1978
Human health		
Drinking water (µg/L)		
USA		
1975	<500	Harrison and
1977	<250	Laxen 1981
1980	<50	EPA 1980; NAS 1980
South Africa	<500	Harrison and Laxen
1981		
Canada, Australia	<50	Demayo et al. 1982
USSR, Japan	<100	Abbasi and
India	10 to <100	Soni 1986

World Health Organization	<100	
Food (mg/kg fresh weight)		
Citrus	<1	NAS 1980
Raw fruits and vegetables	<7	
Fishery products		
Canada	<10	Sirota and Uthe 1977
USA	<0.3	Schmitt et al.
UK		1984
Fish	<2 (~14 dry weight)	Maddock and Taylor 1980
Shellfish	<5 (~35 dry weight)	
Meat, except liver	<0.3	Bunzl and
Liver	<0.8	Kracke 1984
Total diet	<0.3	Czarneski 1985
Daily intake, all sources (mg)		
Unacceptable	>2.3	Nriagu 1978b
Average		
Adult	<0.3	EPA 1980
Child	<0.21	
Urinary Pb levels (μg/L)		
Normal	<80	Nriagu 1978b
Acceptable	80 to 120	
Excessive	120 to 220	
Dangerous	>200	
Blood (μg Pb/L)[g]		
Acceptable (ALAD inhibition, protoporphyrin elevation)	100 to 300	Barth et al. 1973; Nriagu
Anemia, neurobehavioral effects, some poisoning in children	>400	1978b; EPA 1980; Harrison and Laxen 1981
Central nervous system deficits, peripheral neuropathy, intellectual deficits	500 to 700	
Brain structure alterations, encephalopathy	>800	
Life-threatening	>1,000	
Target	<150, maximum 300	
Air (μg Pb/m^3)		
Safe, USA	<1.5 (3-month arithmetic mean)	NAS 1980
Occupational, USA	<50[f]	EPA 1979;

		NAS 1980
Proposed, worldwide	<2	Barrett and
		Howells 1984
Hazardous	2,220	Barth et al. 1973
House paints (mg/L)	<600	EPA 1979
Gasoline (mg/L)		
USA		
Recent	473 to 658[d]	EPA 1979
Proposed	131[e]	
UK		
1972	840	Harrison and
1978	450	Laxen 1981
1981	400	Barrett and
Proposed	150	Howells 1984
West Germany	150	Harrison and Laxen
1981		

[a]Each reference applies to the values in the same row, and in the rows that follow for which no other reference is indicated.

[b]Four-day average, not to be exceeded more than once every 3 years.

[c]One-hour average, not to be exceeded more than once every 3 years.

[d]Equals 1.8 to 2.5 g/gallon.

[e]Equals 0.5 g/gallon.

[f]Average 8-hour period.

[g]Blood Pb levels, usually expressed as µg/deciliter, have been converted to µg/L, for uniformity, in the present work.

The evidence implicating ingestion of spent lead shot as a major cause of mortality in waterfowl and other birds is overwhelming. Moreover, forms of inorganic lead--besides Pb shot or other ingestible-sized Pb objects-- are not known to produce subclinical signs of Pb toxicosis in avian populations. Accordingly, in the 1986 advent of the Pb shot phaseout, steel shot nontoxic zones were established for the protection of bald eagles and waterfowl in 44 States. Possession of shotshells containing Pb shot by hunters of waterfowl in a steel shot zone is now considered a violation of Federal regulations (FWS 1986, 1986a, 1987). By 1991-1992, and thereafter, all uses of Pb shot for hunting waterfowl and coots are to be eliminated nationwide, including Alaska. The conversion to a nontoxic shot zone may be deferred until--but not beyond--the 1991-1992 hunting season in States that demonstrate, through monitoring, compliance with the following criteria: minimum of 100 birds sampled; less than 5% of birds examined having one or more Pb shot in the gizzard; and less than 5% of the birds collected having >2 mg Pb/kg fresh weight in liver, or with >0.2 mg Pb/1 in blood, or with blood protoporphyrin concentrations >0.4 mg/l. In addition, the occurrence of three or more individual specimens confirmed as lead-poisoned during the monitoring year will disqualify the area for deferral (FWS 1986, 1986a, 1987). States may elect to forego monitoring and convert to nontoxic shot zones on a countywide or statewide scheduled or accelerated basis (FWS 1986, 1987).

The level of human exposure in Pb-using industries has been reduced considerably in recent years; associated with this observation is the reduction in Pb content of gasolines, the removal of Pb-based paints for interior household use, and the reduction in Pb content of outside paints (Table 9; Boggess 1977). These actions will undoubtedly prove beneficial in reducing the elevated Pb concentrations now observed in communities of flora and fauna along heavily traveled roads, and in providing additional protection to captive zoo animals and other animals held in enclosures with Pb-painted bars and walls. The decreased use of leaded gasoline has resulted in a significant decline in Pb concentrations in streams (Smith et al. 1987), and in whole body burdens of Pb in starlings collected nationwide, among which the decline was most pronounced in birds from urban areas (White et al. 1977). Continued nationwide monitoring of Pb in fish and wildlife is necessary to determine if this is a continuing downward trend, and also to identify areas of high or potential Pb contamination.

Data for Pb effects on mammalian wildlife are conspicuously absent. In view of the large interspecies differences in Pb responses reported for domestic livestock and laboratory populations of small animals (Table 9), more research is needed to determine if Pb criteria for these groups are applicable to sensitive species of mammalian wildlife.

One of the more insidious effects documented for Pb in warm-blooded organisms is neurobehavioral deficits (including learning impairments) at dose levels producing no overt signs of toxicity, i.e., apparently normal growth and developmental skills, and sometimes, nonelevated blood Pb levels (EPA 1980, 1985; Rice 1985). Behavioral deficits have been reported for young rats when blood Pb levels exceeded 0.1 mg/l, and in children with blood Pb concentrations of 0.4 to 0.5 mg/l (EPA 1980; Rice 1985), and in birds when Pb was administered early in development (Burger and Gochfeld 1985). Recently, behavioral impairment was recorded in 3-year-old monkeys that received 50 or 100 ug Pb/kg BW from birth to age 200 days. Blood Pb levels immediately after exposure, and at time of testing, were 0.15 to 0.25 mg/l (age 200 days), and 0.11 to 0.13 mg/l (age 3 years); this is the first report of behavioral impairment in a primate species at blood Pb concentrations that are considered to be well within the bounds of safety for children (Rice 1985). This subject appears to constitute a high priority research need for wildlife species of concern.

LITERATURE CITED

Abbasi, S.A., and R. Soni. 1986. An examination of environmentally safe levels of zinc (II), cadmium (II) and lead (II) with reference to impact on channelfish *Nuria denricus*. Environ. Pollut. 40A:37-51.

Adams, E.S. 1975. Effects of lead and hydrocarbons from snowmobile exhaust on brook trout (*Salvelinus fontinalis*). Trans. Am. Fish. Soc. 104:363-373.

Anders, E., D.D. Dietz, C.R. Bagnell, Jr., J. Gaynor, M R. Krigman, D.W. Ross, J.D. Leander, and P. Mushak. 1982. Morphological, pharmacokinetic, and hematological studies of lead-exposed pigeons. Environ. Res. 28:344-363.

Anderson, R.V. 1977. Concentrations of cadmium, copper, lead and zinc in thirty-five genera of freshwater macroinvertebrates from the Fox River, Illinois and Wisconsin. Bull. Environ. Contam. Toxicol. 18:345-349.

Anderson, W.L., and S.P. Havera. 1985. Blood lead, protoporphyrin, and ingested shot for detecting lead poisoning in waterfowl. Wildl. Soc. Bull. 13:26-31.

Angell, N.F., and B. Weiss. 1982. Operant behavior of rats exposed to lead before or after weaning. Toxicol. Appl. Pharmacol. 63:62-71.

Aronson, A.L. 1971. Biologic effects of lead in fish. J. Wash. Acad. Sci. 61:124-128.

Backhaus, B., and R. Backhaus. 1986. Is atmospheric lead contributing to mid-European forest decline? Sci. Total Environ. 50:223-225.

Bagley, G.E., and L.N. Locke. 1967. The occurrence of lead in tissues of wild birds. Bull. Environ. Contam. Toxicol. 2:297-305.

Barrett, B., and R. Howells. 1984. Legal control of standards: lead in petrol. Sci. Total Environ. 33:1-13.

Barrett, J., and P.J. Livesey. 1983. Lead induced alterations in maternal behavior and offspring development in the rat. Neurobehav. Toxicol. Teratol. 5:557-563.

Barrett, J., and P.J. Livesey. 1985. Low level lead effects on activity under varying stress conditions in the developing rat. Pharmacol. Biochem. Behav. 22:107-118.

Barth, D., A. Berlin, R. Engel, P. Recht, and J. Smeets (eds.). 1973. Proceedings international symposium. Environmental health aspects of lead. Comis. European Commun., Luxembourg. 1,168 pp.

Beeby, A. 1985. The role of Helix aspersa as a major herbivore in the transfer of lead through a polluted ecosystem. J. Appl. Ecology 22: 267-275.

Behan, M.J., T.B. Kinraide, and W.I. Selser. 1979. Lead accumulation in aquatic plants from metallic sources including shot. J. Wildl. Manage. 43:240-244.

Bellrose, F.C. 1951. Effects of ingested lead shot upon waterfowl populations. Trans. North Am. Wildl. Conf. 16:125-135.

Bellrose, F.C. 1959. Lead poisoning as a mortality factor in waterfowl populations. Illinois Nat. Hist. Surv. Bull. 27:235-288.

Benes, P., M. Cejchanova, and B. Havlik. 1985. Migration and speciation of lead in a river system heavily polluted from a smelter. Water Res. 19:1-6.

Beresford, W.A., M.P. Donovan, J.M. Henninger, and M.P. Waalkes. 1981. Lead in the bone and soft tissues of box turtles caught near smelters. Bull. Environ. Contam. Toxicol. 27:349-352.

Berglind, R., G. Dave, and M.L. Sjobeck. 1985. The effects of lead on aminolevulinic acid dehydratase activity, growth, hemoglobin content, and reproduction in Daphnia magna. Ecotoxicol. Environ. Safety 9: 216-229.

Bernhard, M., and A. Zattera. 1975. Major pollutants in the marine environment. Pages 195-300 in E.A. Pearson and E.D. Frangipane (eds.). Marine pollution and marine waste disposal. Pergamon Press, New York.

Beyer, W.N., and A. Anderson. 1985. Toxicity to woodlice of zinc and lead oxides added to soil litter. Ambio 14:173-174.

Beyer, W. N., and E. J. Cromartie. 1987. A survey of Pb, Cu, Zn, Cd, Cr, As and Se in earthworms and soil from diverse sites. Environ. Monitor. Assess. 8:27-36.

Beyer, W. N., G. W. Miller, and E. J. Cromartie. 1984. Contamination of the 02 soil horizon by zinc smelting and its effect on woodlouse survival. J. Environ. Qual. 18: 247-251.

Beyer, W.N., and J. Moore. 1980. Lead residues in eastern tent caterpillars (Malacosoma americanum) and their host plant (Prunus serotina) close to a major highway. Environ. Entomol. 9:10-12.

Beyer, W.N., O.H. Pattee, L. Sileo, D.J. Hoffman, and B.M. Mulhern. 1985. Metal contamination in wildlife living near two zinc smelters. Environ. Pollut. 38A:63-86.

Beyer, W.N., J.W. Spann, L. Sileo, and J.C. Franson. 1988. Lead poisoning in six captive avian species. Arch. Environ. Contam. Toxicol. 17:121-130.

Birdsall, C.W., C.E. Grue, and A. Anderson. 1986. Lead concentrations in bullfrog Rana catesbeiana and green frog R. clamitans tadpoles inhabiting highway drainages. Environ. Pollut. 4OA:233-247.

Birkhead, M. 1983. Lead levels in the blood of mute swans Cygnus olor on the River Thames. J. Zool. (Lond.) 199:59-73

Bjerre, G.K., and H.H. Schierup. 1985. Uptake of six heavy metals by oat as influenced by soil type and additions of cadmium, lead, zinc and copper. Plant Soil 88:57-69.

Blus, L.J., B.S. Neely, Jr., T.G. Lamont, and B. Mulhern. 1977. Residues of organochlorines and heavy metals in tissues and eggs of brown pelicans, 1969-73. Pestic. Monitor. J. 11:40-53.

Boggess, W.R. (ed.). 1977. Lead in the environment. Natl. Sci. Found. Rep.NSF/RA-770214. 272 pp. Avail. from U.S. Gov. Printing Office, Washington,D.C. 20402.

Bohn, A. 1979. Trace metals in fucoid algae and purple sea urchins near a high Arctic lead/zinc ore deposit. Mar. Pollut. Bull. 10:325-327.

Bollingberg, H., and P. Johansen. 1979. Lead in spotted wolffish, *Anarhichas minor*, near a zinc-lead mine in Greenland. J. Fish. Res. Board Can. 36:1023-1028.

Bolter, E., D. Hemphill, B. Wixson, D. Butherus, and R. Chen. 1973. Geochemical and vegetation studies of trace substances from lead smelting. Pages 79-86 *in* D.D. Hemphill (ed.). Trace substances in environmental health. Vol. VT-. Univ. Missouri, Columbia.

Borgmann, U., O. Kramar, and C. Loveridge. 1978. Rates of mortality, growth, and biomass production of *Lymnaea palustris* during chronic exposure to lead. J. Fish. Res. Board Can. 35:1109-1115.

Boyer, I.J., and V. Di Stefano. 1985. An investigation of the mechanism of lead-induced relaxation of pigeon crop smooth muscle. J. Pharmacol. Exp. Ther. 234:616-623.

Boyer, I.J., D.A. Cory-Slechta, and V. Di Stefano. 1985. Lead induction of crop dysfunction in pigeons through a direct action on neural or smooth muscle components of crop tissue. J. Pharmacol. Exp. Ther. 234:607-615.

Braham, H.W. 1973. Lead in the California sea lion (*Zalophus californianus*). Environ. Pollut. 5:253-258.

Branica, M., and Z. Konrad (eds.). 1980. Lead in the marine environment. Pergamon Press, Oxford, England. 353 pp.

Buerger, T.T., R.E. Mirarchi, and M.E. Lisano. 1986. Effects of lead shot ingestion on captive mourning dove survivability and reproduction. J. Wildl. Manage. 50:1-8.

Bull, K.R., W.J. Avery, P. Freestone, J.R. Hall, D. Osborn, A.S. Cooke, and T. Stowe. 1983. Alkyl lead pollution and bird mortalities on the Mersey estuary, UK, 1979-1981. Environ. Pollut. 31A:239-259.

Bunzl, K., and W. Kracke. 1984. Distribution of ^{210}Pb, ^{210}Po, stable lead and fallout ^{137}Cs in soil, plants and moorland sheep of a heath. Sci. Total Environ. 39:143-159.

Burger, J., and M. Gochfeld. 1985. Early postnatal lead exposure: behavioral effects in common tern chicks (*Sterna hirundo*). J. Toxicol. Environ. Health 16:869-886.

Burrows, G.E. 1981. Lead toxicosis in domestic animals: a review of the role of lead mining and primary lead smelters in the United States. Vet. Human Toxicol. 23:337-343.

Burrows, G.E., and R.E. Borchard. 1982. Experimental lead toxicosis in ponies: comparison of the effects of smelter effluent-contaminated hay and lead acetate. Am. J. Vet. Res. 43:2129-2133.

Carlson, B.L., and S.W. Nielsen. 1985. Influence of dietary calcium on lead poisoning in mallard ducks (*Anas platyrhynchos*). Am. J. Vet. Res. 46:276-282.

CEP. 1979. International conference. Management and control of heavy metals in the environment. CEP Consultants, Edinburgh, UK. 664 pp.

Chasko, G.G., T.R. Hoehn, and P. Howell-Heller. 1984. Toxicity of lead shot to wild black ducks and mallards fed natural foods. Bull Environ. Contam. Toxicol. 32:417-428.

Chau, Y.K., P.T.S. Wong, O. Kramer, G.A. Bengert, R.B. Cruz, J.O. Kinrade, J. Lye, and J.C. Van Loon. 1980. Occurrence of tetraalkyllead compounds in the aquatic environment. Bull. Environ. Contam. Toxicol. 24:265-269.

Chmiel, K.M., and R.M. Harrison. 1981. Lead content of small mammals at a roadside site in relation to the pathways of exposure. Sci. Total Environ. 17:145-154.

Clark, D.R., Jr. 1979. Lead concentrations: bats vs. terrestrial small mammals collected near a major highway. Environ. Sci. Technol. 13:338-341.

Clark, D.R., Jr., A.S. Wenner, and J.F. Moore. 1986. Metal residues in bat colonies, Jackson County, Florida, 1981-1983. Florida Field Natur. 14:38-45.

Clausen, B., K. Elvestad, and 0. Karlog. 1982. Lead burden in mute swans from Denmark. Nord. Vet.-Med. 34:83-91.

Clausen, I.H.S. 1984. Lead (Pb) in spiders: a possible measure of atmospheric Pb pollution. Environ. Pollut. 8B:217-230.

Clemens, E.T., L. Krook, A.L. Aronson, and C.E. Stevens. 1975. Pathogenesis of lead shot poisoning in the mallard duck. Cornell Vet. 65:248-285.

Colle, A., J.A. Grimaud, M. Boucherat, and Y. Manvel. 1980. Lead poisoning in monkeys: functional and histopathological alterations of the kidneys. Toxicology 18:145-158.

Collins, M.F., P.D. Hrdina, E. Whittle, and R.L. Singhal. 1982. Lead in blood and brain regions of rats chronically exposed to low doses of the metal. Toxicol. Appl. Pharmacol. 65:314-322.

Cory-Slechta, D.A., S.T. Bissen, A.M. Young, and T. Thompson. 1981. Chronic postweaning lead exposure and response duration performance. Toxicol. Appl. Pharmacol. 60:78-84.

Cory-Slechta, D.A., B. Weiss, and C. Cox. 1983 Delayed behaviorial toxicity of lead with increasing exposure concentration. Toxicol. Appl. Pharmacol. 71:342-352.

Cory-Slechta, D.A., B. Weiss, and C. Cox. 1985. Performance and exposure indices of rats exposed to low concentrations of lead. Toxicol. Appl. Pharmacol. 78:291-299.

Coughlan, D.J., S.P. Gloss, and J. Kubota. 1986 Acute and sub-chronic toxicity of lead to the early life stages of smallmouth bass (Micropterus dolomieui). Water, Air, Soil Pollut. 28:265-275.

Custer, T.W., J.C. Franson, and O.H. Pattee. 1984. Tissue lead distribution and hematologic effects in American kestrels (Falco sparverius L.) fed biologically incorporated lead. J. Wildl. Dis. 20:39-43.

Czarneski, J.M. 1985. Accumulation of lead in fish from Missouri streams impacted by lead mining. Bull. Environ. Contam. Toxicol. 34:736-745.

Czech, D.A., and E. Hoium. 1984. Some aspects of feeding and locomotor activity in adult rats exposed to tetraethyl lead. Neurobehav. Toxicol. Teratology 6:357-361.

Dallinger, R., and W. Wieser. 1984. Patterns of accumulation, distribution and liberation of Zn, Cu, Cd and Pb in different organs of the land snail Helix pomatia L. Comp. Biochem. Physiol. 79C:117-124.

Davies, P.H., J.P. Goettl, Jr., J.R. Sinley, and N.F. Smith. 1976. Acute and chronic toxicity of lead to rainbow trout Salmo gairdneri, in hard and soft water. Water Res. 10:199-206.

Decker, R.A., and A.M. McDermid, and J.W. Prideaux. 1979. Lead poisoning in two captive king vultures. J. Am. Vet. Med. Assoc. 175:1009.

Demayo, A., M.C. Taylor, K.W. Taylor, and P.V. Hodson. 1982. Toxic effects of lead and lead compounds on human health, aquatic life, wildlife plants, and livestock. CRC Crit. Rev. Environ. Control 12:257-305.

De Ment, S.H., J.J. Chisolm, Jr., J.C. Barker, and J.D. Strandberg. 1986. Lead exposure in an "urban" peregrine falcon and its avian prey. J. Wildl. Dis. 22:238-244.

De Michele, S.J. 1984. Nutrition of lead. Comp. Biochem. Physiol. 78A:401-408.

Deuel, B. 1985. Experimental dosing of northern pintails in California. Calif. Fish Game 71:125-128.

Dieter, M.P. 1979. Blood delta-aminolevulinic acid dehydratase (ALAD) to monitor lead contamination in canvasback ducks (Aythya valisineria). Pages 177-191 in National Academy of Sciences. Animals as monitors of environmental pollutants. Washington, D.C.

Dieter, M.P., and M.T. Finley. 1978. Erythrocyte □-aminolevulinic acid dehydratase activity in mallard ducks: duration of inhibition after lead shot dosage. J. Wildl. Manage. 42:621-625.

Dieter, M.P., and M.T. Finley. 1979. Delta aminolevulinic acid dehydratase enzyme activity in blood, brain, and liver of lead-dosed ducks. Environ. Res. 19:127-135.

Dieter, M.P., M.C. Perry, and B.M. Mulhern. 1976. Lead and PCB's in canvasback ducks: relationship between enzyme levels and residues in blood. Arch. Environ. Contam. Toxicol. 5:1-13.

Dietz, D.D., D.E. McMilland, and P. Mushak. 1979. Effects of chronic lead administration on acquisition and performance of serial position sequences by pigeons. Toxicol. Appl. Pharmacol. 47:377-384.

Di Giulio, R.T., and P.F. Scanlon. 1984. Effects of cadmium and lead ingestion on tissue concentrations of cadmium, lead, copper, and zinc in mallard ducks. Sci. Total Environ. 39:103-110.

Di Giulio, R.T., and P.F. Scanlon. 1985. Heavy metals in aquatic plants, clams, and sediments from the Chesapeake Bay, U.S.A. Implications for waterfowl. Sci. Total Environ. 41:259-274.

Diters, R.W., and S.W. Nielsen. 1978. Lead poisoning of raccoons in Connecticut. J. Wildl. Dis. 14:187-192.

Dodge, R.E., and T.R. Gilbert. 1984. Chronology of lead pollution contained in banded coral skeletons. Mar. Biol. 82:9-13.

Dollahite, J.W., R.L. Younger, H.R. Crookshank, L.P. Jones, and H.D. Petersen. 1978. Chronic lead poisoning in horses. Am. J. Vet. Res. 39:961-964.

Dollard, G.J. 1986. Glasshouse experiments on the uptake of foliar applied lead. Environ. Pollut. 4OA:109-119.

Dorn, C.R., P.E. Phillips, J.O. Pierce, and G.R. Chase. 1974. Cadmium, copper, lead and zinc in bovine hair in the lead belt of Missouri. Bull. Environ. Contam. Toxicol. 11:626-630.

Drifmeyer, J.E., and W.E. Odum. 1975. Lead, zinc and manganese in dredgespoil pond ecosystems. Environ. Conserv. 2:39-43.

Driver, C.J., and R.J. Kendall. 1984. Lead shot ingestion in waterfowl in Washington State, 1978-1979. Northwest Sci. 58:103-107.

Eastin, W.C., Jr., D.J. Hoffman, and C.T. O'Leary. 1983. Lead accumulation and depression of □-aminolevulinic acid dehydratase (ALAD) in young birds fed automotive waste oil. Arch. Environ. Contam. Toxicol. 12:31-35.

Edwards, M.J., and J. Beatson. 1984. Effects of lead and hyperthermia on prenatal growth of guinea pigs. Teratology 30-:413-421.

Edwards, W.C., and B.R. Clay. 1977. Reclamation of rangeland following a lead poisoning incident in livestock from industrial airborne contamination of forage. Vet. Human. Toxicol. 19:247-249.

Eisenreich, S.J., N.A. Metzer, N.R. Urban, and J.A. Robbins. 1986. Response of atmospheric lead to decreased use of lead in gasoline. Environ. Sci. Technol. 20:171-174.

Eisler, R. 1977. Toxicity evaluation of a complex metal mixture to the softshell clam *Mya arenaria*. Mar. Biol. 43:265-276.

Eisler, R. 1981. Trace metal concentrations in marine organisms. Pergamon Press, New York. 687 pp.

Eisler, R. 1984. Trace metal changes associated with age of marine vertebrates. Biol. Trace Elem. Res. 6:165-180.

EPA. 1972. Helena Valley, Montana, area environmental pollution study. U.S. Environ. Protection Agency Rep. AP-91. 179 pp. Avail. from U.S. Environ. Protection Agency, Office of Air Programs, Research Triangle Park, North Carolina 27711.

EPA. 1979. The health and environmental impacts of lead and an assessment of a need for limitations. U.S. Environ. Protection Agency Rep. 560/2-79-001. 494 pp.

EPA. 1980. Ambient water quality criteria for lead. U.S. Environ. Protection Agency Rep. 440/5-80-057. 151 pp. Avail. from Natl. Tech. Infor. Serv., 5285 Port Royal Road, Springfield, Virginia 22161.

EPA. 1985. Ambient water quality criteria for lead - 1984. U.S. Environ. Protection Agency Rep. 440/5-84-027. 81 pp. Avail. from Natl. Tech. Infor. Serv., 5285 Port Royal Road, Springfield, Virginia 22161.

Eskildsen, J., and P. Grandjean. 1984. Lead exposure from lead pellets: age-related accumulation in mute swans. Toxicol. Lett. 21:225-229.

Everard, M., and P. Denny. 1984. The transfer of lead by freshwater snails in Ullswater, Cumbria. Environ. Pollut. 35A:299-314.

Everard, M., and P. Denny. 1985. Flux of lead in submerged plants and its relevance to a freshwater system. Aquatic Bot. 21:181-193.

Fantin, A.M.B., A. Franchini, E. Ottaviani, and L. Benedetti. 1985. Effect of pollution on some freshwater species. II. Bioaccumulation and toxic effects of experimental lead pollution on the ganglia in *Viviparus ater* (Mollusca, Gastropoda). Basic Appl. Histochem. 29:377-387.

Fayed, S.I., and H.I. Abd-El-Shafy. 1985. Accumulation of Cu, Zn, Cd, and Pb by aquatic macrophytes. Environ. Int. 11:77-87.

Feierabend, J.S., and O. Myers. 1984. A national summary of lead poisoning in bald eagles and waterfowl. 90 pp. Avail. from National Wildlife Federation, 1412 Sixteenth St. NW, Washington, D.C. 20036.

Feierabend, J.S., and A.B. Russell (eds.). 1986. Lead poisoning in wild waterfowl - a workshop. National Wildlife Federation, 1412 Sixteenth St. NW, Washington, D.C. 139 pp.

Fimreite, N. 1984. Effects of lead shot ingestion in willow grouse. Bull. Environ. Contam. Toxicol. 33:121-126.

Finley, M.T., and M.P. Dieter. 1978. Influence of laying on lead accumulation in bone of mallard ducks. J. Toxicol. Environ. Health 4:123-129.

Finley, M.T., M.P. Dieter, and L.N. Locke. 1976. Sublethal effects of chronic lead ingestion in mallard ducks. J. Toxicol. Environ. Health 1:929-937.

Flegal, A.R. 1985. Lead in a pelagic food chain. Pages 83-90 *in* J. Salanki (ed.). Heavy metals in water organisms. Symposia Biologica Hungarica, Vol. 29. Akademiai Kiado, Budapest, Hungary.

Fleming, W.J. 1981. Environmental metal residues in tissues of canvasbacks. J. Wildl. Manage. 45:508-511.

Forbes, R.M., and G.C. Sanderson. 1978. Lead toxicity in domestic animals and wildlife. Pages 225-227 *in* J.O. Nriagu (ed.). The biogeochemistry of lead in the environment. Part B. Biological effects. Elsevier/NorthHolland Biomedical Press, Amsterdam.

Forsyth, D.S., W.D. Marshall, and M.C. Collette. 1985. Interaction of alkyllead salts with avian eggs. J. Environ. Sci. Health 2OA:177-191.

Fowler, M.E. 1975. Toxicities in exotic and zoo animals. Vet. Clinics North Amer. 5:685-698.

Fowler, S.W. 1977. Trace elements in zooplankton particulate products. Nature (Lond.) 269:51-53..

Franson, J.C., and T.W. Custer. 1982. Toxicity of dietary lead in young cockerels. Vet. Human Toxicol. 24:421-423.

Franson, J.C., G.M. Haramis, M.C. Perry, and J.F. Moore. 1986. Blood protoporphyrin for detecting lead exposure in canvasbacks. Pages 32-37 in J.S. Feierabend and A.B. Russell (eds.). Lead poisoning in wild waterfowl - a workshop. National Wildlife Federation, 1412 Sixteenth St. NW, Washington, D.C.

Franson, J.C., L. Sileo, O.H. Pattee, and J.F. Moore. 1983. Effects of chronic dietary lead in American kestrels (Falco sparverius). J. Wildl. Dis. 19:110-113.

Frape, D.L., and J.D. Pringle. 1984. Toxic manifestations in a dairy herd consuming haylage contaminated by lead. Vet. Rec. 114:615-616.

Fraser, J. 1980. Acclimation to lead in the freshwater isopod Asellus aquaticus. Oecologia 45:419-420.

Friedland, A.J., and A.H. Johnson. 1985. Lead distribution and fluxes in a high-elevation forest in northern Vermont. J. Environ. Qual. 14:332-336.

Friend, M. 1985. Interpretation of criteria commonly used to determine lead poisoning problem areas. U.S. Fish Wildl. Serv., Fish Wildl. Leafl. 2. 4 PP-

FWS. 1986. Migratory bird hunting; availability of a final supplemental environmental impact statement (SEIS) on the use of lead shot for hunting migratory birds in United States. Federal Register 51(124):23443-23447.

FWS. 1986a. Use of lead shot for hunting migratory birds in the United States. Final supplemental environmental impact statement. 535 + xx pp. Avail. from U.S. Fish Wildlife Service, Office of Migratory Bird Management, Washington, D.C. 20240.

FWS. 1987. Migratory bird hunting; zones in which lead shot will be prohibited for the taking of waterfowl, coots and certain other species in the 1987-88 hunting season. Federal Register 52(139):27352-27368.

Gale, N. L., E. Bolter, and B.G. Wixson. 1976. Investigation of Clearwater Lake as a potential sink for heavy metals from lead mining in southeast Missouri. Pages 95-106 in D.D. Hemphill (ed.). Trace substances in environmental health. Vol. X. Univ. Missouri, Columbia.

Geist, C.R., S.W. Balko, M.E. Morgan, and R. Angiak. 1985. Behavioral effects following rehabilitation from postnatal exposure to lead acetate. Percep. Motor Skills 60:527-536.

Getz, L.L., L.B. Best, and M. Prather. 1977a. Lead in urban and rural song birds. Environ. Pollut. 12:235-239.

Getz, L.L., L. Verner, and M. Prather. 1977b. Lead concentrations in small mammals living near highways. Environ. Pollut. 13:151-157.

Getz, L.L., A.W. Haney, R.W. Larimore, J.W. McNurney, H.V. Leland, P.W. Price, G.L. Rolfe, R.L. Wortman, J.L. Hudson, R.L. Solomon, and K.A. Reinbold. 1977c. Transport and distribution in a watershed ecosystem. Pages 105-134 in W.R. Boggess, (ed.). Lead in the environment. Natl. Sci. Found. Rep. NSF/RA-770214. Avail. from U.S. Govt. Printing Office, Washington, D.C. 20402.

Gietzen, D.W., and D.E. Wooley. 1984. Acetylcholinesterase activity in the brain of rat pups and dams after exposure to lead via the maternal water supply. Neurotoxicology 5:235-246.

Gilmartin, J.E., D.K. Alo, M.E. Richmond, C.A. Bache, and D.J. Lisk. 1985. Lead in tissues of cats fed pine voles from lead-arsenate treated orchards. Bull. Environ. Contam. Toxicol. 34:291-294.

Gish, C.D., and R.E. Christensen. 1973. Cadmium, nickel, lead and zinc in earthworms from roadside soil. Environ. Sci. Technol. 7:1060-1072.

Gjerstad, K.O., and I. Hanssen. 1984. Experimental lead poisoning in willow ptarmigan. J. Wildl. Manage. 48:1018-1022.

Goede, A.A., and P. de Voogt. 1985. Lead and cadmium in waders from the Dutch Wadden Sea. Environ. Pollut. 37A:311-322.

Goldsmith, C.D., and P.F. Scanlon. 1977. Lead levels in small mammals and selected invertebrates associated with highways of different traffic densities. Bull. Environ. Contam. Toxicol. 17:311-316.

Goodman, G.T., and T.M. Roberts. 1971. Plants and soils as indicators of metals in the air. Nature (Lond). 231:287-292.

Gould, E., and R.A. Greig. 1983. Short-term low-salinity response in lead-exposed lobsters, *Homarus americanus* (Milne Edwards). J. Exp. Mar. Biol. Ecol. 69:283-295.

Graham, D.L. 1972. Trace metal levels in intertidal mollusks of California. Veliger 14:365-372.

Grue, C.E., D.J. Hoffman, W.N. Beyer, and L.P. Franson. 1986. Lead concentrations and reproductive success in European starlings *Sturnus vulgaris* nesting within highway roadside verges. Environ. Pollut. 42A:157-182.

Grue, C.E., T.J. O'Shea, and D.J. Hoffman. 1984. Lead concentrations and reproduction in highway-nesting barn swallows. Condor 86:383-389.

Haegele, M.A., R.K. Tucker, and R.H. Hudson. 1974. Effects of dietary mercury and lead on eggshell thickness in mallards. Bull. Environ. Contam. Toxicol. 8:5-11.

Hall, R.A., E.G. Zook, and G.M. Meaburn. 1978. National Marine Fisheries Service survey of trace elements in the fishery resource. U.S. Dep. Commerce, NOAA Tech. Rep. NMFS SSRF-721. 313 pp.

Hall, S.L., and F.M. Fisher, Jr. 1985. Lead concentrations in tissues of marsh birds: relationship of feeding habits and grit preference to spent shot ingestion. Bull. Environ. Contam. Toxicol. 35:1-8.

Hamir, A.N. 1981. Lead poisoning of dogs in Australia. Veety Rec. 108:438-439.

Hamir, A.N., N.D. Sullivan, and P.D. Handson. 1982. The effects of age and diet on the absorption of lead from the gastrointestinal tract of dogs. Aust. Vet. J. 58:266-268.

Hardisty, M.W., S. Kartar, and M. Sainsbury. 1974. Dietary habits and heavy metal concentrations in fish from the Severn Estuary and Bristol Channel. Mar. Pollut. Bull. 5:61-63.

Harrison, P.D., and M.I. Dyer. 1984. Lead in mule deer forage in Rocky Mountain National Park, Colorado. J. Wildl. Manage. 48:510-517.

Harrison, R.M., W.R. Johnston, J.C. Ralph, and S.J. Wilson. 1985. The budget of lead, copper and cadmium for a major highway. Sci. Total Environ. 46:137-145.

Harrison, R.M., and D.P.H. Laxen. 1981. Lead pollution. Causes and control. Chapman and Hall, New York. 168 pp.

Hastings, L., H. Zenick, P. Succop, T.J. Sun, and R. Sekeres. 1984. Relationship between hematopoietic parameters and behaviorial measures in lead-exposed rats. Toxicol. Appl. Pharmacol. 73:416-422.

Haux, C., and A. Larrson. 1982. Influence of inorganic lead on the biochemical blood composition in the rainbow trout, *Salmo gairdneri*. Ecotoxicol. Environ. Saf. 6:28-34.

Haux, C., A. Larsson, G. Lithner, and M.L. Sjobeck. 1986. A field study of physiological effects on fish in lead-contaminated lakes. Environ. Toxicol. Chem. 5:283-288.

Hayashi, M. 1983. Lead toxicity in the pregnant rat. I. The effect of high-level lead on δ-aminolevulinic acid dehydratase activity in maternal and fetal blood or tissues. Environ. Res. 30:152-160.

Hejtmancik, M.R., Jr., E.B. Dawson, and B.J. Williams. 1982. Tissue distribution of lead in rat pups nourished by lead-poisoned mothers. J. Toxicol. Environ. Health 9:77-86.

Heyraud, M., and R.D. Cherry. 1979. Polonium-210 and lead-210 in marine food chains. Mar. Biol. 52:227-236.

Hill, E.F., and M.B. Camardese. 1986. Lethal dietary toxicities of environmental contaminants and pesticides to Coturnix. U.S. Fish Wildl. Serv., Fish Wildl. Tech. Rep. 2. 147 pp.

Hodson, P.V. 1976. δ-amino levulinic acid dehydratase activity of fish blood as an indicator of a harmful exposure to lead. J. Fish. Res. Board Can. 33:268-271.

Hodson, P.V., B.R. Blunt, D.J. Spry, and K. Austen. 1977. Evaluation of erythrocyte δ-amino levulinic acid dehydratase activity as a short-term indicator in fish of a harmful exposure to lead. J. Fish. Res. Board Can. 34:501-508.

Hodson, P.V., D.G. Dixon, D.J. Spry, D.M. Whittle, and J.B. Sprague. 1982. Effect of growth rate and size of fish on rate of intoxication by waterborne lead. Can. J. Fish. Aquat. Sci. 39:1243-1251.

Hodson, P.V., J.W. Hilton, B.R. Blunt, and S.J. Slinger. 1980. Effects of dietary ascorbic acid on chronic lead toxicity to young rainbow trout (*Salmo gairdneri*). Can. J. Fish. Aquat. Sci. 37:170-176.

Hodson, P.V., and D.J. Spry. 1985. Effect of sulfite dechlorination on the accumulation of waterborne lead by rainbow trout (*Salmo gairdneri*). Can. J. Fish. Aquat. Sci. 42:841-844.

Hoffman, D.J., J.C. Franson, O.H. Pattee, C.M. Bunck, and A. Anderson. 1985a. Survival, growth, and accumulation of ingested lead in nestling American kestrels (*Falco sparverius*). Arch. Environ. Contam. Toxicol. 14:89-94.

Hoffman, D.J., J.C. Franson, O.H. Pattee, C.M. Bunck, and H.C. Murray. 1985b. Biochemical and hematological effects of lead ingestion in nestling American kestrels (*Falco sparverius*). Comp. Biochem. Physiol. 80C:431-439.

Hoffman, D.J., O.H. Pattee, S.N. Wiemeyer, and B. Mulhern. 1981. Effects of lead shot ingestion on δ-aminolevulinic acid dehydratase activity, hemoglobin concentration, and serum chemistry in bald eagles. J. Wildl. Dis. 17:423-431.

Holcombe, G.W., D.A. Benoit, E.N. Leonard, and J.M. McKim. 1976. Long-term effects of lead exposure on three generations of brook trout (*Salvelinus fontinalis*). J. Fish. Res. Board Can. 33:1731-1741.

Holl, W., and R. Hampp. 1975. Lead and plants. Residue Rev. 54:79-111.

Hong, J.S., H.A. Tilson, P. Hudson, S.F. Ali, W.E. Wilson, and V. Hunter. 1983. Correlation of neurochemical and behaviorial effects of triethyl lead chloride in rats. Toxicol. Appl. Pharmacol. 69:471-479.

Hopkin, S.P., G.N. Hardisty, and M.H. Martin. 1986. The woodlouse *Porcellio scaber* as a 'biological indicator' of zinc, cadmium, lead and copper pollution. Environ. Pollut. 11B:271-290.

Hopkin, S.P., and M.H. Martin. 1984. Assimilation of zinc, cadmium, lead and copper by the centipede *Lithobius variegatus* (Chilopoda). J. Appl. Ecol. 21:535-546.

Hopkins, A. 1970. Experimental lead poisoning in the baboon. Brit. J. Indust. Med. 27:130-140.

Howard, D.R., and R.A. Braum. 1980. Lead poisoning in a dairy herd. Annu. Proc. Am. Assoc. Vet. Lab. Diag. 23:53-58.

Hudson, R.H., R. K. Tucker, and M.A. Haegele. 1984. Handbook of toxicity of pesticides to wildlife. U.S. Fish Wildl. Serv. Resour. Publ. 153. 90 pp.

Hunter, B., and G. Wobeser. 1980. Encephalopathy and peripheral neuropathy in lead-poisoned mallard ducks. Avian Dis. 24:169-178.

Ireland, M.P. 1977. Lead retention in toads *Xenopus laevis* fed increasing levels of lead in contaminated earthworms. Environ. Pollut. 12:85-92.

Irmer, U., I. Wachholz, H. Schafer, and D.W. Lorch. 1986. Influence of lead on *Chlamydomonas reinhardii* Danegard (Volvocales, Chlorophyta): accumulation, toxicity and ultrastructural changes. Environ. Exper. Bot. 26:97-105.

Jacobson, E., J. W. Carpenter, and M. Novilla. 1977. Suspected lead toxicosis in a bald eagle. J. Am. Vet. Med. Assoc. 171:952-954.

Janssen, D.L., J.E. Oosterhuis, J.L. Allen, M.P. Anderson, D.G. Kelts, and S.N. Wiemeyer. 1986. Lead poisoning in free-ranging California condors. J. Am. Vet. Med. Assoc. 189:1115-1117.

Jenkins, D.W. 1980. Biological monitoring of trace metals. Vol. 2. Toxic trace metals in plants and animals of the world. Part II. U.S. Environ. Protection Agency Rep. 600/3-80-091:619-778.

Johansson-Sjobeck, M.J., and A. Larsson. 1979. Effects of inorganic lead on delta-aminolevulinic acid dehydratase activity and hematological variables in the rainbow trout, *Salmo gairdneri*. Arch. Environ. Contam. Toxicol. 8:419-431.

Johnson, M.S., H. Pluck, M. Hutton, and G. Moore. 1982. Accumulation and renal effects of lead in urban populations of feral pigeons, *Columba livia*. Arch. Environ. Contam. Toxicol. 11:761-767.

Jordan, J. S., and F. C. Bellrose. 1951. Lead poisoning in wild waterfowl. Illinois Nat. Hist. Surv. Div., Biol. Notes 26. 27 pp.

Kania, D. M., and T. Nash. 1986. Impact of lead on migratory birds in Missouri. Unpubl. rep. 41 pp. Available from U.S. Fish Wildl. Serv.,P.O. Box 1506, Columbia, Missouri 65205.

Kaplan, H.M., T.J. Anrholt, and J.E. Payne. 1967. Toxicity of lead nitrate solutions for frogs (*Rana pipiens*). Lab. Animal Care 17:240-246.

Kendall, R.J. and C.J. Driver. 1982. Lead poisoning in swans in Washington State. J. Wildl. Dis. 18:385-387.

Kendall, R.J., G.W. Norman, and P.F. Scanlon. 1984. Lead concentrations in ruffed grouse collected from southwestern Virginia. Northwest Sci. 58:14-17.

Kendall, R.J., and P.F. Scanlon. 1981. Effects of chronic lead ingestion on reproductive characteristics of ringed turtle doves *Streptopelia risoria* and on tissue lead concentrations of adults and their progeny. Environ. Pollut. 26A:203-213.

Kendall, R.J., and P.F. Scanlon. 1982. The toxicology of ingested lead acetate in ringed turtle doves *Streptopelia risoria*. Environ. Pollut. 27A:255-262.

Kendall, R.J., and P.F. Scanlon. 1083. Histologic and ultrastructural lesions of mourning doves (*Zenaida macroura*) poisoned by lead shot. Poult. Sci. 62:952-956.

Kendall, R.J., and P.F. Scanlon. 1984. The toxicology of lead shot ingestion in ringed turtle doves under conditions of cold exposure. J. Environ. Pathol. Toxicol. 5:183-192.

Kendall, R.J., and P.F. Scanlon. 1981. Histology and ultrastructure of kidney tissue from ringed turtle doves that ingested lead. J. Environ. Pathol. Toxicol. Oncol. 6:85-96.

Kendall, R.J., P.F. Scanlon, and R.T. Di Giulio. 1982. Toxicology of ingested lead shot in ringed turtle doves. Arch. Environ. Contam. Toxicol. 11:259-263.

Kendall, R.J., H.P. Veit, and P.F. Scanlon. 1981. Histological effects and lead concentrations in tissues of adult male ringed turtle doves that ingested lead shot. J. Toxicol . Environ. Health 8:649-658.

Kimmel, C.A., L.D. Grant, C.S. Sloan, and B.C. Gladen. 1980. Chronic low-level lead toxicity in the rat. 1. Maternal toxicity and perinatal effects. Toxicol. Appl. Phamacol. 56:28-41.

King, K.A., and E. Cromartie. 186. Mercury, cadmium, lead, and selenium in three waterbird species nesting in Galveston Bay, Texas, USA. Colon. Waterbirds 9:90-94.

Kirby, R.E., H.H. Obrecht III, and M.C. Perry. 1983. Body shot in Atlantic brant. J. Wildl. Manage. 47: 27-530.

Kisseberth, W.C., J.P. Sundberg, .W. Nyboer, J.D. Reynolds, S.C. Kasten, and V.R. Beasley. 1984. Industrial lead contamination of an Illinois wildlife refuge and indigenous small mammals. J. Am. Vet. Med. Assn. 185:1309-1313.

Knight, H.D., and R.G. Burau 19 3. Chronic lead poisoning in horses. J. Am. Vet. Med. Assoc. 162:781-786.

Knowlton, M.F., T.P. Boyle, and J.R. Jones. 1983. Uptake of lead from aquatic sediment by submersed macrophytes and crayfish. Arch. Environ. Contam. Toxicol. 12:535-541.

Kobayashi, N. 1971. Fertilized sea urchin eggs as an indicatory material for marine pollution bioassay, preliminary experiments. Publ. Seto Mar. Biol. Lab. (Japan) 18:379-406.

Kober, T.E., and G.P. Cooper. 1976. Lead competitively inhibits calcium-dependent synoptic transmission in the bullfrog sympathetic ganglion. Nature (Lond). 262:704-705.

Krishnayya, N.S.R., and S.J. Bedi., 1986. Effect of automobile lead pollution in *Cassia tora* L. and *Cassia occidentalis* L. Environ. Pollut. 4OA:2 1-226.

Krajnovic-Ozretic, M., and B. Ozretic. 1980. The ALA-D activity test in lead exposed grey mullet *Mugil auratus*. Mar. Ecol. Prog. Ser. 3:187-191.

Kumar, S., and S.C. Pant. 1984.. Comparative effects of the sublethal poisoning of zinc, copper and lead on the gonads of the teleost *Puntius conchonius* Ham. Toxicol. Lett. 23:189-194.

Kwatra, M.S., B.S. Gill, R. Singh,, and M. Singh. 1986. Lead toxicosis in buffaloes and cattle in Punjab. Indian J. Anim. Sci. 56:412-413.

Lansdown, R., and W. Yule (eds.). 1986. Lead toxicity. History and environmental impact. Johns Hopkins Univ. Press, Baltimore, Maryland. 286 pp.

Lassen, E.D., and W.B. Buck. 1979. Experimental lead toxicosis in swine. Am. J. Vet. Res. 40:1359-1364.

Levander, O.A. 1979. Lead toxicity and nutritional deficiencies. Environ. Health Perspec. 29:115-125.

Locke, L. N., and G. E. Bagley. 1967. Lead poisoning in a sample of Maryland mourning doves. J. Wildl. Manage. 31:515-518.

Locke, L. N., G. E. Bagley, D. N. Frickie, and L. T. Young. 1969. Lead poisoning and aspergillosis in an Andean condor. J. Am. Vet. Med. Assoc. 155:1052-1056.

Locke, L. N., G. E. Bagley, and H. D. Irby. 1966. Acid-fast intranuclear inclusion bodies in the kidneys of mallards fed lead shot. Bull. Wildl. Dis. Assoc. 2:127-131.

Locke, L.N., S.M. Kerr, and D. Zoromski. 1982. Case report - lead poisoning in common loons (*Gavia immer*). Avian Dis. 26:392-396.

Longcore, J.R., L.N. Locke, G.E. Bagley, and R. Andrews. 1974a. Significance of lead residues in mallard tissues. U.S. Fish Wildl- Serv. Spec. Sci. Rep. - Wildl. 182. 24 pp.

Longcore, J.R., R. Andrews, L.N. Locke, G.E. Bagley, and L.T. Young. 1974b. Toxicity of lead and proposed substitute shot to mallards. U.S. Fish Wildl. Serv. Spec. Sci. Rep.- Wildl. 183. 23 pp.

Longcore, J.R., P.O. Corr, and H.E. Spencer, Jr. 1982. Lead shot incidence in sediments and waterfowl gizzards from Merrymeeting Bay, Maine. Wildl. Soc. Bull. 10:3-10.

Lowe, T.P., T.W. May, W.G. Brumbaugh, and D.A. Kane. 1985. National Contaminant Biomonitoring Program: concentrations of seven elements in freshwater fish, 1978-1981. Arch. Environ. Contam. Toxicol. 14:363-388.

Lumeij, J.T. 1985. Clinicopathologic: aspects of lead poisoning in birds: a review. Vet. Q. 7:133-138.

Lumeij, J.T., W.T.C. Wolvekamp, G.M. Bron-Dietz, and A.J.H Schotman. 1985. An unusual case of lead poisoning in a honey buzzard (*Pernis apivorus*).Vet. Q. 7:165-168.

Luoma, S.N., and G.W. Bryan. 1978. Factors controlling the availability of sediment-bound lead to the estuarine bivalve *Scrobicularia plana*. J. Mar. Biol. Assoc. U.K. 58:793-802.

Macdonald, J.W., C.J. Randall, H.M. Ross, G.M. Moon, and A.D. Ruthven. 1983. Lead poisoning in captive birds of prey. Vet. Rec. 113:65-66.

Mackay, D.W., W. Halcrow, and I. Thornton. 1972. Sludge dumping in the Firth of Clyde. Mar. Pollut. Bull. 3:7-10.

Maddock, B.G., and D. Taylor. 1980. The acute toxicity and bioaccumulation of some lead alkyl compounds in marine animals. Pages 233-261 *in* M. Branica and Z. Konrad (eds.). Lead in the marine environment. Pergamon Press, Oxford, England.

Mahaffey, K.R., J.I. Rader, J.M. Schaefer, and S.N. Kramer. 1980. Comparative toxicity to rats of lead acetate from food or water. Bull. Environ. Contam. Toxicol. 25:541-546.

Marchetti, R. 1978. Acute toxicity of alkyl leads to some marine organisms. Mar. Pollut. Bull. 9:206-20.

Marcus, A.H. 1985. Multicompartment kinetic models for lead. I. Bone diffusion models for long-term retention. Environ. Res. 36:441-458.

Martin, W.E., and P.R. Nickerson. 1973. Mercury, lead, cadmium, and arsenic residues in starlings - 1971. Pestic. Monitor. J. 7:67-72.

Massaro, T.F., G.D. Miller, and, E.J. Massaro. 1986. Low-level lead exposure affects latent learning in the rat. Neurobehav. Toxicol. Teratol. 8:109-113.

May, T.W., and G.L. McKinney. 1981. Cadmium, lead, mercury, arsenic, and selenium concentrations in freshwater fish, 1976-77 - National Pesticide Monitoring Program. Pestic. Monitor. J. 15:14-38.

McDonald, L.J. 1986. Suspected lead poisoning in an Amazon parrot. Can. Vet. J. 27:131-134.

McLean, R.O., and A.K. Jones. 1975. Studies of tolerance to heavy metals in the flora of the rivers Ystwyth and Clarach, Wales. Freshwater Biol. 5:431-444.

Melhuus, A., K.L. Seip, H.M. Seip, and S. Mykelstad. 1978. A preliminary study of the use of benthic algae as biological indicators of heavy metal pollution in Sorfjorden, Norway. Environ. Pollut. 15:101-107.

Mierau, G.W., and B.E. Favara. 1975. Lead poisoning in roadside populations of deer mice. Environ. Pollut. 8:55-64.

Mudge, G.P. 1983. The incidence and significance of ingested lead pellet poisoning in British wildfowl. Biol. Conserve 27:333-372.

Mulhern, B.M., W.L. Reichel, L.N. Locke, T.G. Lamont, A. Belisle, E. Cromartie, G.E. Bagley, and R.M. Prouty. 1970. Organochlorine residues and autopsy data from bald eagles 1966-68. Pestic. Monitor. J. 4:141-144.

Mykkanen, H.M., M.C. Lancaster, J. W. T. Dickerson. 1982. Concentrations of lead in the soft tissues of male rats during a long-term dietary exposure. Environ. Res. 28:147-153.

Narbaitz, R., 1. Marino, and K. Sarkar. 1985. Lead-induced early lesions in the brain of the chick embryo. Teratology 32:389-396.

NAS. 1980. Lead in the human environment. National Academy of Sciences; Washington, D.C. 525 pp.

Nation, J.R., D.E. Clark, A.E. Bourgeois, and J.K. Rogers. 1982. Conditioned suppression in the adult rat following chronic exposure to lead. Toxicol. Lett. 14:63-67.

Niethammer, K.R., R.D. Atkinson, T.S. Baskett, and F.B. Samson. 1985. Metals in riparian wildlife of the lead mining district of southeastern Missouri. Arch. Environ. Contam. Toxicol. 14:213-223.

NRCC. 1973. Lead in the Canadian environment. Natl. Res. Coun. Canada Publ. BY73-7 (ES). 116 pp. Avail. from Publications, NRCC/CNRC, Ottawa, Canada KIA OR6.

Nriagu, J.O. (ed.). 1978a. The biogeochemistry of lead in the environment. Part A. Ecological cycles. Elsevier/North Holland Biomedical Press, Amsterdam. 422 pp.

Nriagu, J.O. (ed.). 1978b. The biogeochemistry of lead in the environment. Part B. Biological effects. Elsevier/North Holland Biomedical Press, Amsterdam. 397 pp.

Ogilvie, D.M., and A.H. Martin 1982. Aggression and open-field activity of lead-exposed mice. Arch. Environ. Contam. Toxicol. 11:249-252.

Ohi, G., H. Seki, K. Akiyama, and H. Yagyu. 1974. The pigeon, a sensor of lead pollution. Bull. Environ. Contam . Toxicol. 12:92-98.

Osborn, D., W.J. Eney, and K.R Bull 1983. The toxicity of trialkyl lead compounds to birds. Environ. Pollut. 31A:261-275.

Osweiler, G.D., and G.A. Van Gelder. 1978. Epidemiology of lead poisoning in animals. Pages 143-177 in F.W. Oehme (ed.). Toxicity of heavy metals in the environment. Part 1. Marcel Dekker, New York.

Ozoh, P.T.E. 1980. Effect of lead on pigment pattern formation in zebrafish (Brachydanio rerio). Bull. Environ. Contam. Toxicol. 24:276-282.

Pain, D. J. 1987. Lead poisoning in waterfowl: an investigation of sources and screening techniques. Ph.D. thesis, Oxford University, England. 335 pp.

Pain, D. J., and B. A. Rattner. 1988. Mortality and hematology associated with the ingestion of one number four lead shot in black ducks, Anas rubripes. Bull. Environ. Contam. Toxicol. 40:159-164.

Pattee, O.H. 1984. Eggshell thickness and reproduction in American kestrels exposed to chronic dietary lead. Arch. Environ. Contam. Toxicol. 13:29-34.

Pattee, O.H., and S.K. Hennes 1983. Bald eagles and waterfowl: the lead shot connection. Trans. N. Am. Wildl. Nat. Resour. Conf. 48:230-237.

Pattee, O.H., S.N. Wiemeyer, B.M. Mulhern, L. Sileo, and J.W. Carpenter. 1981. Experimental lead-shot poisoning in bald eagles. J. Wildl. Manage. 45:806-810.

Perry, M. C., and J. W. Artmann. 1979. Incidence of embedded and ingested shot in oiled ruddy ducks. J. Wildl. Manage. 43:266-269.

Perry, M. C., and P. H. Geissler. 1980. Incidence of embedded shot in canvasbacks. J. Wildl. Manage. 44:888-894.

Peter, F., and G. Strunc. 1983. Effect of ingested lead on concentration of blood and tissue lead in rabbits. Clin. Biochem. 16:202-205.

Prause, B., E. Rehm, and M. Schulz-Baldes. 1985. The remobilization of Pb and Cd from contaminated edge spoil after dumping in the marine environment. Environ. Technol. Lett. 6:261-266.

Rai, R., and M.A. Qayyum. 1984. Haematological responses in a freshwater fish to lead poisoning. J. Environ. Biol. 5:53-56.

Raymond, R.B., and R.B. Forbes. 11975. Lead in hair of urban and rural small mammals. Bull. Environ. Contam. Toxicol. 13:551-553.

Redig, P.T., C.M. Stowe, D.M. Barnes, and T.D. Arent. 1980. Lead toxicosis in raptors. J. Am. Vet. Med. Assoc. 177:941.

Reichel, W.L., S.K. Schmeling, E. Cromartie, T.E. Kaiser, A.J. Krynitsky, T.G. Lamont, B.M. Mulhern, R.M. Prouty, C.J. Stafford, and D.M. Swineford. 1984. Pesticide, PCB, and lead residues and necropsy data for bald eagles from 32 states - 1978-81. Environ. Monitor. Assess. 4:395-403.

Reichert, W.L., D.A. Federighi, and D.C. Malins. 1979. Uptake and metabolism of lead and cadmium in coho salmon (*Oncorhynchus kisutch*). Comp. Biochem. Physiol. 63C:229-234.

Reish, D.J., and T.V. Gerlinger. 1964. The effects of cadmium, lead, and zinc on survival and reproduction in the polychaetous annelid *Neanthes arenaceodentata* (F. Nereididae). Pages 383-389 *in* P.A. Hutchings (ed.) Proceedings of the first international polychaete conference. Sydney. Linnean Soc. N.S.W., Australia.

Rice, D.C. 1985. Chronic low-lead exposure from birth produces deficits in discrimination reversal in monkeys. Toxicol. Appl. Pharmacol. 77:201-210.

Rivkin, R.B. 1979. Effects of lead on the growth of the marine diatom *Skeletonema costatum*. Mar. Biol. 50:239-247.

Robel, R.J., C.A. Howard, M.S. Udevitz, and B. Curnutte, Jr. 1981. Lead contamination in vegetation, cattle dung, and dung beetles near an interstate highway, Kansas. Environ. Entomol. 10:262-263.

Roberts, R.D., M.S. Johnson, and M. Hutton. 1978. Lead contamination of small mammals from abandoned metalliferous mines. Environ. Pollut. 15:61-69.

Roberts, T.M., P.B. Heppleston, and R.D. Roberts. 1976. Distribution of heavy metals in tissues of the common seal. Mar. Pollut. Bull. 7:194-196.

Rolfe, G.L., and K.A. Reinbold. 1977. Environmental contamination by lead and other heavy metals. Volume I: introduction and summary. Univ. Illinois, Inst. Environ. Studies, Urbana-Champaign. 120 pp.

Rombaugh, P.J. 1985. The influence of the zona radiata on the toxicities of zinc, lead, mercury, copper and silver ions to embryos of steelhead trout *Salmo gairdneri*. Comp. Biochem. Physiol. 82C:115-117.

Ruhling, A., and G. Tyler. 1968 An ecological approach to the lead problem. Bot. Notiser. 121:321 342.

Sadiq, M. 1985. Uptake of cadmium, lead and nickel by corn grown in contaminated soils. Water Air Soil Pollut. 26:185-190.

Sanderson, G.C., and F.C. Bellrose. 1986. A review of the problem of lead poisoning in waterfowl. Illinois Nat. Hist. Surv., Spec. Publ. 4. 34 pp.

Schlick, E., K. Mengel, and K.D. Friedberg. 1983. The effect of low lead doses in vitro and in vivo on the *d-ala-d* activity of erythrocytes, bone marrow cells, liver and brain of the mouse. Arch. Toxicol. 53:193-205.

Schmitt, C.J., F.J. Dwyer, and S.E. Finger. 1984. Bioavailability of Pb and Zn from mine tailings as indicated by erythrocyte ☐-aminolevulinic acid dehydratase (ALA-D) activity in suckers (Pisces: Catostomidae). Can. J. Fish. Aquat. Sci. 41:1030-104).

Schmitt, C. J., and S. E. Finger. 1987. The effects of sample preparation on measured concentrations of eight elements in edible tissues of fish from streams contaminated by lead mining. Arch. Environ. Contam. Toxicol. 16:185-207.

Schulz-Baldes, M. 1972. Toxicity and accumulation of lead in the common mussel *Mytilus edulis* in laboratory experiment. Mar. Biol. 16:226-229.

Schulz-Baldes, M. 1974. Lead uptake from sea water and food, and lead loss in the common mussel, *Mytilus edulis*. Mar. Biol. 25:177-193.

Schulz-Baldes, M., and R.A. Lewin. 1976. Lead uptake in two marine phytoplankton organisms. Biol. Bull. 150:118-127.

Scoullos, M.J. 1986. Lead in coastal sediments: the case of the Elefsis Gulf, Greece. Sci. Total Environ. 49:199-219.

Seeliger, U., and P. Edwards. 1977. Correlation coefficients and concentration factors of copper and lead in seawater and benthic algae. Mar. Pollut. Bull. 8:16-19.

Settle, D. M., and C. C. Patterson. 1980. Lead in albacore: guide to lead pollution in Americans. Science 207:1167-1176.

Sharma, S., and K.C. Kanwar. 1985. Reproductive performance in mice following lead administration. Res. Bull. Panjab Univ. 36:389-394.

Sheppard, C.R.C., and D.J. Bellamy. 1974. Pollution of the Mediterranean around Naples. Mar. Pollut. Bull. 5:42-44.

Sileo, L., and W.N. Beyer. 1985. Heavy metals in white-tailed deer living near a zinc smelter in Pennsylvania. J. Wildl. Dis. 21:289-296.

Sileo, L., and S. I. Fefer. 1987. Paint chip poisoning of Laysan albatross at Midway Atoll. J. Wildl. Dis. 23:432-437.

Sirota, G.R., and J.F. Uthe. 1977. Determination of tetraalkyl lead compounds in biological materials. Anal. Chem. 49:823-825.

Sleet, R.B., and J.H. Soares, Jr. 1979. Some effects of Vitamin E deficiency on hepatic xanthine dehydrogenase activity, lead, and ☐ tocopherol concentrations in tissues of lead-dosed mallard ducks. Toxicol. Appl. Pharmacol. 47:71-78.

Smith, G.J., and O.J. Rongstad. 1982. Small mammal heavy metal concentrations from mined and control sites. Environ. Pollut. 28A:121-134.

Smith, R. A., R. B. Alexander, and P. G. Wolman. 1987. Water-quality trends in the Nation's rivers. Science 235:1607-1615.

Spehar, R.L., R.L. Anderson, and J.T. Fiandt. 1978. Toxicity and bioaccumulation of cadmium and lead in aquatic invertebrates. Environ. Pollut. 15:195-208.

Srebocan, E., and B. A. Rattner. 1988. Heat exposure and the toxicity of one number four lead shot in mallards, *Anas platyrhynchos*. Bull. Environ. Contam. Toxicol. 40:165-169.

Stendell, R.C. 1980. Dietary exposure of kestrels to lead. J. Wildl. Manage. 44:527-530.

Stendell, R.C., J.W. Artmann, and E. Martin. 1980. Lead residues in sora rails from Maryland. J. Wildl. Manage. 44:525-527.

Stendell, R.C., R.I. Smith, K.P. Burnham, and R.E. Christensen. 1979. Exposure of waterfowl to lead: a nationwide survey of residues in wing bones of seven species, 1972-73. U.S. Fish Wildl. Serv. Spec. Sci. Rep. -Wildl. 223. 12 pp.

Stewart, J., and M. Schulz-Baldes. 1976. Long-term lead accumulation in abalone (*Haliotis* spp.) fed on lead-treated brown algae (*Egregia laevigata*). Mar. Biol. 36:19-24.

Stone, C.L., and M.R.S. Fox. 1984. Effects of low levels of dietary lead and iron on hepatic RNA, protein, and minerals in young Japanese quail. Environ. Res. 33:322-332.

Stone, W.B., and S.A. Butkas. 1978. Lead poisoning in a wild turkey. N.Y. Fish Game J. 25:169.

Stournaras, C., G. Weber, H. P. Zimmermann, K.H. Doenges, and H. Faulstich. 1984. High cytotoxicity and membrane permeability of Et_3Pb^+ in mammalian and plant cells. Cell Biochem. Func. 2:213-216.

Street, M. 1983. The assessment of mortality resulting from the ingestion of spent lead shot by mallard wintering in South East England. Congr. Int. Fauna Cinegetica y Silvestre 15 (1981):161-167.

Sundstrom, R., K. Muntzing, H. Kalimo, and P. Sourander. 1985. Changes in the integrity of the blood-brain barrier in suckling rats with low dose lead encephalopathy. Acta Neuropathol. 68:1-9.

Szymczak, M.R., and W.J. Adrian. 1978. Lead poisoning in Canada geese in southeast Colorado. J. Wildl. Manage. 42:299-306.

Tachon, P., A. Laschi, J.P. Briffaux, and G. Brain. 1983. Lead poisoning in monkeys during pregnancy and lactation. Sci. Total Environ. 30:221-229.

Ter Haar, G.I. 1970. Air as a source of lead in edible crops. Environ. Sci. Technol. 4:226-229.

Tsuchiya, K. 1979. Lead. Pages 451-484 *in* L. Friberg, G.E. Nordberg, and V.B. Vouk (eds.). Handbook on the toxicology of metals. Elsevier/NorthHolland Biomedical Press, Amsterdam.

Turner, R.S., A.H. Johnson, and D. Wang. 1985. Biogeochemistry of lead in McDonalds Branch watershed, New Jersey Pine Barrens. J. Environ. Qual. 14:305-314.

Udevitz, M.S., C.A. Howard, R.J. Robel, and B. Curnutte, Jr. 1980. Lead contamination in insects and birds near an interstate highway, Kansas. Environ. Entomol. 9:35-36.

Varanasi, U., and D.J. Gmur. 1978. Influence of water-borne and dietary calcium on uptake and retention of lead by coho salmon (*Oncorhynchus kisutch*). Toxicol. Appl. Pharmacol. 46:65-75.

Veit, H.P., R.J. Kendall, and P.F. Scanlon. 1983. The effect of lead shot ingestion on the testes of adult ringed turtle doves (*Streptopelia risoria*). Avian Dis. 27:442-452.

Vighi, M. 1981. Lead uptake and release in an experimental trophic chain.Ecotoxicol. Environ. Safety 5:177-193.

Walsh, D.F., B.L. Berger, and J.R. Bean. 1977. Mercury, arsenic, lead, cadmium, and selenium residues in fish, 1971-73 - National PesticideMonitoring Program. Pestic. Monitor. J. 11:5-34.

Walsh, T.J., and H.A. Tilson. 1984. Neurobehaviorial toxicology of the organoleads. Neurotoxicology 5:67-86.

Ward, N.I., and R.R. Brooks. 1979. Lead levels in wool as an indication of lead in blood of sheep exposed to automotive emissions. Bull. Environ. Contam. Toxicol. 21:403-408.

Way, C.A., and G.D. Schroder. 1982. Accumulation of lead and cadmium in wild populations of the commensal rat *Rattus norvegicus*. Arch. Environ. Contam. Toxicol. 11:407-417.

Wetmore, A. 1919. Lead poisoning in waterfowl. U.S. Dep. Agricul. Bull. 793. 12 pp.

White, D.H., J.R. Bean, and J.R. Longcore. 1977. Nationwide residues of mercury, lead, cadmium, arsenic, and selenium in starlings, 1973. Pestic. Monitor. J. 11:35-39.

White, D.H., K.A. King, C.A. Mitchell, and B.M. Mulhern. 1986. Trace elements in sediments, water, and American coots (*Fulica americana*) at a coal-fired power plant in Texas, 1979-1982. Bull. Environ. Contam. Toxicol. 36:376-383.

White, D.H., and R.C. Stendell. 1977. Waterfowl exposure to lead and steel shot on selected hunting areas. J. Wildl. Manage. 41:469-475.

White, J.R., and C.T. Driscoll. 1985. Lead cycling in an acidic Adirondack lake. Environ. Sci. Technol. 19:1182-1187.

Wide, M. 1985. Lead exposure on critical days of fetal life affects fertility in the female mouse. Teratology 32:375-380.

Wiener, J.G., G.A. Jackson, T.W. May, and B.A. Cole. 1984. Longitudinal distribution of trace elements (As, Cd, Cr, Hg, Pb, and Se) in fishes and sediments in the upper Mississippi River. Pages 139-170 *in* J.G. Wiener, R.V. Anderson, and D.R. McConville (eds.). Contaminants in the upper Mississippi River. Butterworth Publ., Stoneham, Massachusetts.

Windingstad, R.M., S.M. Kerr, L.P. Locke, and J.J. Hurt. 1984. Lead poisoning of sandhill cranes (*Grus canadensis*). Prairie Nat. 16:21-24.

Wobeser, G.A. 1981. Diseases of wild waterfowl. Plenum Press, New York. 300 pp.

Wong, P.T.S., Y.K. Chau, O. Kramar, and G.A. Bengert. 1981. Accumulation and depuration of tetramethyllead by rainbow trout. Water Res. 15:621-625.

Wong, P.T.S., B.A. Silverberg, Y.K. Chau, and P.V. Hodson. 1978. Lead and the aquatic biota. Pages 279-342 *in* J.O. Nriagu (ed.). The biogeochemistry of lead in the environment. Part B. Biological effects. Elsevier/North Holland Biomedical Press, Amsterdam.

Yeung, G.L. 1978. The influence of lead, an environmental pollutant on metamorphosis of *Rana utricularia* (Amphibia: Ranidae). Arkansas Acad. Sci. Proc. 32:83-86.

Zaroogian, G.E., G. Morrison, and J.F. Heltshe. 1979. *Crassostrea virginica* as an indicator of lead pollution. Mar. Biol. 52:189-196.

Zirkin, B.R., R. Gross, and L.L. Ewing. 1985. Effects of lead acetate on male rate reproduction. Pages 13 - 145 *in* F. Hamburger and A.M. Goldberg (eds.). Concepts in toxicology. Vol. 3. In vitro embryotoxicity and teratogenicity tests. Karger, Basel, Switzerland.

Zmudzki, J., G.R. Bratton, C. Womac, and L. Rowe. 1983. Lead poisoning in cattle: reassessment of the minimum toxic oral dose. Bull. Environ. Contam. Toxicol. 30:435-441.

Zmudzki, J., G.R. Bratton, C. Womac, and L.D. Rowe. 1984. The influence of milk diet, grain diet, and method of dosing on lead toxicity in young calves. Toxicol. Appl. Pharmacol. 76:490-497.

Zook, B.C., R.M. Sauer, and F.,M. Garner. 1972. Lead poisoning in captive wild animals. J. Wildl. Dis. 8:264-272.

Zwank, P.J., V.L. Wright, P.M. Shealy, and J.D. Newsom. 1985. Lead toxicosis in waterfowl on two major wintering areas in Louisiana. Wildl. Soc. Bull. 13:17-26.